DISCARDED

Famous Biographies for Young People

FAMOUS AUTHOR-ILLUSTRATORS FOR YOUNG PEOPLE

by Norah Smaridge

ILLUSTRATED WITH PHOTOGRAPHS

Dodd, Mead & Company · New York

ISBN: 0-396-06831-6
Library of Congress Catalog Card Number: 73-6033
Printed in the United States of America
by Vail-Ballou Press, Inc., Binghamton, N. Y.

Grateful acknowledgment is made to the following for permission to reprint the material indicated:

From *Edward Lear: The Life of a Wanderer* by Vivian Noakes. Copyright © 1969 by Vivian Noakes. Reprinted by permission of Houghton Mifflin Company.

From *The Secret Door* by Covelle Newcomb. Copyright 1946 by Covelle Newcomb. Reprinted by permission of Dodd, Mead & Company, Inc.

From *The Art of Beatrix Potter*. Copyright © 1955 by Frederick Warne and Company, Inc. Reprinted by permission of Frederick Warne and Company, Inc.

From *Beatrix Potter* by Marcus Crouch. Copyright © 1960 by The Bodley Head, Ltd. Reprinted by permission of Henry Z. Walck, Inc.

From *The Journal of Beatrix Potter*. Copyright © 1966 by Frederick Warne and Company, Inc. Reprinted by permission of Frederick Warne and Company, Inc.

From *Rabbit Hill* by Robert Lawson. Copyright 1944 by Robert Lawson, © 1972 by John Boyd. Reprinted by permission of The Viking Press, Inc.

From *The Tough Winter* by Robert Lawson. Copyright 1954 by Robert Lawson. Reprinted by permission of The Viking Press, Inc.

From *Wanda Gág: The Story of an Artist* by Alma Scott. Copyright © 1949 by the University of Minnesota. Reprinted by permission of the University of Minnesota Press.

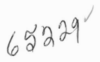

65229

FOR MARIA H. ARNDT
"LENI"
with love and appreciation

CONTENTS

CONTENTS

EDWARD LEAR

*E*DWARD LEAR is usually thought to be the inventor of the limerick. Actually, the origin of this five-line nonsense rhyme is obscure, but Lear, with his fervid imagination and his talent for coining non-words, popularized the limerick and brought it to perfection in such rhymes as:

> There was an old person of Ware
> Who rode on the back of a bear;
> When ask'd, "Does it trot?"
> He said, "Certainly not!
> It's a Moppsikon Floppsikon bear!"

Lear was born on May 12, 1812, in Holloway, a fashionable village to the north of London. His home, Bowman Lodge, was large and elegant, with rustic views of fields and woods. Jeremiah Lear, his father, was a wealthy stockbroker whose wife, Ann, bore him twenty children. Edward, the youngest, was handed over to his 26-year-old sister, Ann, when he was four. This rejection by his mother was deeply felt.

Ann was devoted to the sensitive, plain little boy. She taught him his lessons, read to him from the Bible, mythology, and the poets of the time, and—best of all—showed him how to draw butterflies, birds, and flowers. Edward's fa-

11

vorite hideaway was the little "painting room" set aside for the children.

All through his life, Edward suffered from epilepsy, a hereditary disease. The attacks began when he was very young, and he sometimes had several in a day. He was so secretive about his affliction that no one except his family suspected that he lived in constant dread of a recurrence. His illness meant that he was often alone, living in his imagination and developing into a somewhat odd, but gentle and lovable, character.

Lear grew up in the age of the great landscape painters, like John Constable and William Turner, and was early interested in their art. He paid frequent visits to his married sister, Sarah, in Arundel, Sussex, and was introduced to many artists in that paintable countryside. But if he dreamed of becoming a painter himself, his hopes received an early setback. At seventy, his father retired on a limited income and Edward, at fifteen, was told to make his own way.

He was enterprising enough. From the modest rooms which he shared with Ann in an unfashionable district of London, he went out to give drawing lessons to private pupils. He also did colored posters for shopkeepers and made "morbid disease drawings for hospitals and certain doctors."

He soon found a happier way to earn his living. He began to draw birds, working for Prideaux Selby, an ornithological draughtsman who brought out several fine volumes of British birds not long after Audubon began painting the birds of North America.

In 1830, Lear started on his own first book and was given permission to study and draw the birds in London's new

Zoological Gardens. Attracted by their brilliant plumage
and excitable personalities, he confined himself to parrots.
"Sitting in the parrot house, he was obviously regarded as
something of a curiosity himself," says his most recent biographer, Vivien Noakes, "for the visitors came and stared at
him and his work, and as a change from drawing birds he
would make indignant sketches of the bonneted ladies and
startled gentlemen who peered at him."

Though he produced twenty folios of drawings and won
an enviable reputation before he was twenty, Lear did not
finish drawing all the parrots. He found the work time con-
suming and costly, and he turned, instead, to illustrating and
to working for the British Museum.

In 1832, he was invited to draw the animals in the private
menagerie owned by Lord Stanley of Knowsley Hall, Lanca-
shire. He spent the next four years on the estate, content and
comfortable but keeping much to himself. "The uniform ap-
athetic tone assumed by lofty society irks me *dreadfully*," he
wrote to a friend, "nothing I long for half so much as to gig-
gle heartily and hop on one leg down the great gallery—but
I dare not."

However, he loved the high-spirited children who filled
the nurseries and they reveled in his company. He amused
them by making up nonsense rhymes and drawing grotesque
animals and outlandish people. He invented unimaginable
places with outrageous names, like the Hill Orfeltugg, the
Valley of Verrikwier, the Lake of Oddgrow and the Great
Gromboolian Plain.

By the time he said good-bye to Knowsley Hall, his eyesight and his health were in poor condition. So Lord Stanley, always his friend and benefactor, offered to pay for him

to go to Rome to study painting and build up his health.

Leaving England in the summer of 1837, Lear stayed in Rome for ten years, making occasional visits to London and going on summer trips in Italy and Sicily. His rooms in the Via del Babbuino (Street of the Baboon) were cheap and the neighborhood was congenial, filled with painters and sculptors and with English residents and visitors. He soon found patrons among the English. "I have 2 or 3 water coloured drawings already ordered," he wrote to Ann, then living in Brussels, "so I shall not starve."

Everywhere there were scenes to paint—the strange, dark lake of Lemi, cradled in a hollow of the Alban Hills; the Campagna at sunset, a purple sea in which the city floated like a mirage; the blue hills where Tivoli drowsed among its olives and vines. Before he left Italy, Lear had enough drawings for two books of lithographs.

In 1845, he returned to England for a long stay. He visited Ann, went to Knowsley, worked on the illustrations for his travel books—and suddenly decided to prepare his nonsense rhymes for publication.

Eighteen hundred and forty-six was a memorable year. He published two volumes of his *Illustrated Excursions in Italy,* brought out *Gleanings from the Menagerie at Knowsley Hall,* and—most important for his future fame—published *A Book of Nonsense,* seventy limericks in two volumes.

Fearing that the author-illustrator of such a flippant book would not be taken seriously as an artist, Lear used the pen name Derry-down-Derry. This led to all sorts of rumors. Some readers said that the Earl of Derby (formerly Lord Stanley) was the author of *A Book of Nonsense.* Others said that the illustrations were caricatures of prominent people and that the poems had political meanings.

"Nonsense!" said Lear. And nonsense it was. His hilarious rhymes, his jaunty birds, and bouncing humans were his own invention, produced for the delight of small friends. When a second, enlarged edition appeared in 1861, the book was so popular that Lear was proud to put his name on the title page.

It was the *Illustrated Excursions,* however, that brought him to the attention of the young Queen Victoria, who engaged him to give her twelve drawing lessons. An entry in her diary for June 15, 1846, shows her satisfaction with her new teacher. "Had a drawing lesson from Mr. Lear, who sketched before me and teaches remarkably well, in landscape painting in water colours . . ."

Lear made another stay in Italy but left it in 1848 when revolution threatened. For fifteen months he toured the Mediterranean, continuing to Egypt and Palestine. Then, in 1889, he went back to England, thinking that he might settle there.

Good fortune awaited him. A Mrs. Warner, friend of the Lear family, had died, leaving him a legacy of five hundred pounds. The balance of her fortune went to "perpetual widows." "I thought directly I heard of the matter that I would marry one of the 30 viddies," Lear wrote to a friend, tongue-in-cheek, "only it occurred to me that she would not be a viddy any more if I married her."

In 1850, although he was thirty-seven, Lear began to study at the Royal Academy Schools. His attendance was probably short. To help keep himself and pay his fees, he published *Journals of a Landscape Painter in Greece and Albania* and

Journals of a Landscape Painter in Southern Calabria and the Kingdom of Naples. During this time one of his paintings, "Claude Lorraine's House on the Tiber," was accepted by the Royal Academy, the first to be thus honored.

From then on, he led a hard-working, satisfying life, often comfortably off but sometimes, because of his generosity to others, briefly in debt. Always a welcome guest, he spent his summers at his friends' country homes, happiest when there were children to entertain.

Winters, because of his precarious health, meant moving to warmer climates. From 1854 to 1855 he wintered on the Nile, and journeyed successively to Corfu, Malta, and Rome, finally building himself a villa at San Remo. When he was over sixty, with the help of Lord Northbrook, then governor-general, he saw a large part of India.

Throughout his life, he was always in touch with his sister Ann. When she died, in 1861, Lear was desolate. Unable to bear his loneliness, he went from friend to friend, until the worst of his grief dulled and he was able to work again. He toyed, as he had sometimes done, with the idea of marriage, but decided that it was unfair to ask any woman to marry an epileptic.

He was fortunate in his friends. There was Frank Lushington, an English barrister whom he met in Malta, very different from Lear in temperament but deeply loved. There was the poet laureate, Alfred Tennyson, and his wife and sons. There was Chichester Fortescue, an unwilling politician, brilliant, sensitive, and appreciative of Lear's talents. And there were artists galore, in whose bohemian company Lear felt at ease, although he knew how to conduct himself in wealthy and aristocratic circles.

Toward the end of 1870, Lear brought out *Nonsense Songs, Stories, Botany and Alphabets,* a collection of drawings and poems originally written, like Beatrix Potter's picture-stories, for the amusement of young friends. It includes that prime favorite, "The Owl and the Pussy-Cat," which opens with a beguiling hint of adventure to come:

> The Owl and the Pussy-Cat went to sea
> In a beautiful pea-green boat:
> They took some honey, and plenty of money
> Wrapped up in a five-pound note.

Laughable Lyrics, the last of Lear's nonsense books to be published in his lifetime, came out in 1877. Like "The Owl and the Pussy-Cat" and "The History of the Seven Families of the Lake Pipple-Popple," these lyric poems are, says Vivien Noakes, "songs of wandering, but now the emphasis is on looking back to a time of happiness that has gone for ever."

In 1880, Lear had to build a new house; a huge hotel had risen just below the Villa Emily, his home in San Remo, blocking off the view and ruining the light in his studio. "My new land has only the road and the Railway between it and the sea," he wrote to Emily Tennyson, "so unless the Fishes begin to build, or Noah's Ark comes to an Anchor below the site, the new Villa Eduardo cannot be spoiled."

The last task that Lear undertook was a set of about two hundred drawings from his travels, to illustrate Tennyson's poems. He did not live to complete it. By seventy-four he was an invalid, crippled with rheumatism and totally blind in his right eye.

> He only said, "I'm very weary,
> The rheumatiz he said,
> He said, it's awful dull & dreary,
> I think I'll go to bed,"

he wrote to himself in the third person, in his diary.

On January 29, 1888, Edward Lear died peacefully, to be remembered less for his painting than for the exuberance of his nonsense poems and the comical exaggeration of his illustrations. No less a critic than John Ruskin placed *A Book of Nonsense* first in a list of "a hundred delectable volumes of contemporary literature."

KATE GREENAWAY

So QUAINT and timeless are the fashions in which Kate Greenaway, English artist and illustrator, clothed her storybook characters that today, more than seventy years after her death, "Kate Greenaway" styles are hailed with delighted recognition. They are worn not only by child actors of the stage and screen but by scores of small children whose mothers appreciate their simplicity and charm.

A living painter of babyhood and childhood, Kate herself scarcely realized the extent of her success. Yet it was phenomenal, because the sum total of her work was small; what she mainly did was to draw Christmas cards, illustrate toy books, and produce a number of dainty water colors. That she became a household word is due to the appeal she made, almost unconsciously, to adults as well as children.

The second of four children, Kate Greenaway was born on March 17, 1846, in Hoxton, a district of London where fine cabinet makers had their workshops. Her father, John Greenaway, was a wood engraver of note. Her mother, Elizabeth Jones, was a gentle but dauntless woman; when her husband met with reverses, she promptly moved her family to the more commercial district of Islington and opened a shop to sell fancy goods and children's clothing.

It was probably in this shop that Kate developed her precocious interest in child fashions, an interest which eventually led her away from Victorian styles to the picturesque country clothes of the 1800's. As a very small girl, Kate began to observe precisely, storing away in her memory such items as "a dark-red pelerine, with three rows of narrow velvet round the cape . . . a drab plush bonnet, trimmed with chenille and red strings . . . a little grey cloth jacket scalloped at the edge . . . a grey squirrel muff."

Kate was a lovable, self-contained child who lived much in her imagination. "There was always something more—behind and beyond everything—to me; the golden spectacles were very big," she wrote to a friend. But there were down-to-earth pleasures, too. Visits to Grandma Jones, a lively old lady "fond of shrewd sayings and full of interesting information." There was Aunt Mary, a wood engraver like Papa, who fed the children sumptuously and read to them from *Pilgrim's Progress* and *Why the Sea Became Salt*. There was Aunt Thorne's rambling garden where, to a little girl unusually sensitive to color, the overgrown nasturtiums were "the gaudiest of the gaudy . . . to be admired beyond everything."

And even for shy Kate, parties were a delight, especially the Twelfth Night party, with its splendid cake and a drawing for king and queen of the festivities. But even better were the days when Papa came home early and whisked them off to the theater "with its fascinating smell of oranges and gas, the scraping of violins, and all the mysterious titillations of the expectant senses. . . ."

When Kate was five and a half, the family moved to a larger house and store, and she and her sister Fanny were allowed, within limits, to walk by themselves in the neighborhood streets. They gazed with admiration at the display in the print shop, and with awe at the lurid chalk pictures drawn by the one-legged pavement artist. And at the corner of Wellington Street, there were often side shows—Punch and Judy, or tightrope walkers, or tumblers leaping and somersaulting.

Indoors were other pleasures. Kate suddenly discovered that she could read, and read she did, everything from penny fairy-tale books to the plays of Shakespeare. She had families of dolls, some wooden creatures with tacked-on clothing; others, china beauties which she dressed herself. "They took their walks abroad on the mantelpiece. Their hats were made of tiny straw plaits trimmed with china ribbons and the fluffy down culled from feathers which had escaped from the pillows."

Through annual vacations at the farm of an old servant in the village of Rolleston, fourteen miles from the nearest large town, Kate learned to know the country as intimately as the city. She became familiar with the animals and the great variety of birds—peacocks, guinea fowl, turkeys, pigeons, and others. She rode to market in a green cart drawn by a brown pony, or paid formal visits "in a high dogcart with a spanking horse named Jack."

Because of the lack of good, affordable neighborhood schools for girls, Kate's early education was perfunctory, sometimes consisting of a few lessons a week from a visiting governess. She spent most of her time drawing, and her parents, sensing that she was talented, sent her to evening art classes when she was twelve. She made such progrsss that she was soon promoted to the day classes at Canonbury House where, at fifteen, she won first prize for six color designs for tiles.

Although drawing from casts, following diagrams, and making studies in light and shade were anathema to Kate, she worked diligently, winning many medals and prizes. She even added to her study hours, taking Life Classes at Heatherley's, a well-known London art school, and later at the newly opened Slade School. She and a friend, Elizabeth Thompson, were such tireless students that they bribed the custodian to lock them in after class ended so that they could put in overtime.

Yet all this time Kate was longing to paint as she pleased. "Flowers, trees drenched with sunshine, romantic maidens, heroic youths, these were what she wanted," says Covelle Newcombe in *The Secret Door*. And, at twenty-two, she took a first step in this direction with "Kilmeny," a water-color illustration of a legend. She also produced "Six Little Drawings on Wood," a miniature set of fairy scenes exhibited at the Dudley Gallery.

The drawings were purchased by the Reverend W. J. Loftie, who used them in *People's Magazine,* which he edited. He became her trusted friend. Helping her in a practical way to solve the difficulty which she had in using color, he presented her with a manual of color harmony which Kate studied carefully. On his recommendation, she also visited the National Gallery to study portraits in color, and the British Museum to pore over illuminated manuscripts.

In 1875, Kate began to contribute illustrations to *Little Folks,* an excellent monthly magazine for children. But her first popular success was a valentine for Marcus Ward and Company, a card which sold twenty-five thousand copies in its first week. This was followed by a series of Christmas cards and child pictures, in all of which Kate dressed the characters in quaint and old-world costumes of her own devising.

Marcus Ward was at first hesitant about these costumes, thinking that people might prefer something more familiar. But the public enjoyed the novelty of Kate Greenaway's conceptions, and her first Christmas card was an instant success. It showed "a pretty little girl in winter dress—a redingote and cape of carnation-red, trimmed with beaver, a beaver tippet and muff, and a beaver bonnet lined with silk and topped with a small panache of plumes."

Marcus Ward feared that his young designer would get into a rut, but Kate was determined to go her own way, and she did. Successfully, for she was soon receiving more commissions than she could fill. In 1866, she exhibited her own water colors at the Dudley Gallery, and in 1877 began to draw for the *Illustrated London News*. But except for her water colors, little of her work was signed.

Her debut as an author-illustrator came soon after she showed some of her poems to Edmund Evans, a color printer who brought out the toy books of such famous contemporary illustrators as Walter Crane and Randolph Caldecott. Mr. Evans was much taken by the naive charm of:

> Five little sisters walking in a row;
> Now, isn't that the best way for little girls to go?
> Each had a round hat, each had a muff,
> And each had a new pelisse of soft green stuff.

Five little marigolds standing in a row;
Now, isn't that the best way for marigolds to grow?
Each with a green stalk, and all the five had got
A bright yellow flower, and a new red pot.

The poems were published, with Kate's own illustrations, in a delectable little book which she titled *Under the Window.* It was acclaimed at once. "In time," said the *Saturday Review,* "the hands of children will wear away, and their pencils and paint-brushes will deface Miss Kate Greenaway's beautiful, fantastic and dainty work." From then on, Kate's name became a household word, not only in England, but in Europe and America.

Under the Window had a stunning effect on children's fashions. Mothers rushed to copy the fur-trimmed redingotes, the frilly aprons, the starched pinafores and farm smocks of Kate's boys and girls. The French called this vogue *Greenwaisme,* "the graceful mode which has already gained the provinces and from wealthy quarters has penetrated into the suburbs." The fashionable colors, too, were pure Kate Greenaway—pale blue, rose pink, apple green, buttercup, lilac, and lemon.

Unfortunately, Kate's style and subjects were widely, and often crudely, imitated. Manufacturers applied her figures and designs to dress materials, chintz, wallpaper, fans, vases, even tiny coffins. In Budapest, potters in the Royal and Imperial Factory traced her flowers and cherubic babies onto plates and teacups.

During 1879–1880, Kate continued her illustrating and brought out two more of her own books, *The Little Folks' Painting Book* and *Kate Greenaway's Birthday Book for Children.* The latter prompted the novelist, Robert Louis

Stevenson, to try his hand at writing poetry for children, so we have Kate to thank for the classic *A Child's Garden of Verses.*

January 7, 1880, was a red letter day for Kate. She received a charming letter from the eminent critic and author, John Ruskin. This was the start of a correspondence which was to last until Ruskin's final illness. Although Kate did not meet him in person until 1882, their friendship developed quickly and included his household.

In Ruskin, Kate found the critic she needed. Beginning with a request that she would try to draw some "actual piece of nature (however little) as it really is," he guided her sympathetically but firmly during their correspondence and exchange of visits.

In 1880, Kate became acquainted with Frederick Locker-Lampson, the author, and his family, through whom she met Robert Browning, the poet, and the family of Alfred Tennyson, England's poet laureate. For a time, she enjoyed a whirl of parties and social life, but she soon found them distracting and returned to her work and her quiet days.

In the following year she was very prolific. Among her productions was Kate Greenaway's *Mother Goose,* hailed as the children's classic of the century. "There was simply no end to the charm of *Mother Goose,*" says Covelle Newcomb, ". . . the children, the white cottages with pink roofs, red shutters and lettuce-green fences; the most enchanting schoolhouse in nursery lore; trim hedges, gay gardens; nooks and corners of village streets; tender little vistas of the English countryside. . . ."

Ruskin, too, had praised the book unreservedly. "You are fast becoming . . . the helpfullest in showing me there are yet living souls on earth who can see beauty and peace and goodwill among men—and rejoice in them. . . . ," he wrote.

During her childhood, Kate had often dreamed of riding in a royal carriage to visit a princess. Now her dream came true. At a tea party in her honor in Buckingham Palace, Kate met the Crown Princess, eldest daughter of Queen Victoria, and drew enchanting little impromptu pictures for her children. The Princess, later the Empress Fredericka of Germany, became a patron for life, buying Kate's pictures for herself and her friends, and accepting autographed Greenaway books with gracious notes of acknowledgment.

In 1883, Kate published her first *Almanack,* which was followed by three others. Tiny books, illustrated with charm and humor, they contained a strange mixture of fact and fancy and were enormously popular. They led, however, to another Greenaway boom, with more imitations of Kate's work. This so appalled Ruskin that he delivered a lecture in Oxford on Kate Greenaway's genius which assured her a perpetual place in English art.

Ruskin, however, did not always approve of Kate's books. Her floral dictionary, *Language of Flowers,* 1884, he found sentimental and wishy-washy. Had she "nothing to paint with but starch and camomile tea," he wondered. But he thought *Mavor's Spelling Book* "ever so nice," although he asked, "Do children ever learn to spell that way?" Fired by his question, Kate next produced her *Alphabet,* of which twenty-five thousand copies were quickly sold.

She next won Ruskin's admiration with *Marigold Garden,* which tenderly recaptures the small, daily events of childhood. But neither Ruskin nor the critics liked *A Apple Pie,*

1886, complaining of its red-lettered titles and large pictures. Children loved it, however, and it remains a nursery favorite to this day.

When Ruskin's health began to fail, necessitating stays abroad and gradually putting an end to his letters and visits, Kate fell prey to doubts and discouragement. The "New Art" arrived; pictures became impressionistic or abstract, and Kate found this dismaying. "Oh, I went to the New English Art Club yesterday," she wrote to Ruskin, *such* productions! . . . They are to my mind all very ugly rough sketches, and they think nothing of leaving out the head or body of any one if that isn't where they want it." Kate herself fell out of fashion. For nine years, she wrote no book of her own, although she had many commissions for miniatures and bookplates.

In 1898, 127 of her pictures were exhibited at the Fine Art Society Gallery. Sixty-six were sold, but these were the least expensive and Kate felt the show a failure.

Although it was expected, the news of Ruskin's death on January 20, 1900, stunned her. "I feel it very much," she wrote to M. H. Spielmann, later her biographer, "for he was a great friend—and there is no one else like him."

Trying to lose herself in her work, Kate found that there were still many things she wanted to do. But no one encouraged her to do them, and no publisher asked for a book.

She was seriously thinking of turning to dress designing when her own health began to deteriorate. By 1901, she was so frail that she was unable to accept an offer of a position that would have been very congenial, the editorship of a new chilren's magazine.

Kate Greenaway died quietly on November 6, 1901. The

poet Austin Dobson wrote a tender farewell to the gentle author-illustrator, titling it simply "K.G."

> Farewell, kind heart. And if there be
> In that unshored Immensity
> Child-Angels, they will welcome thee.
>
> Clean-souled, clear-eyed, unspoiled, discreet,
> Thou gav'st thy gifts to make Life sweet,—
> These shall be flowers about thy feet!

Child-angels and flowers would surely be a fitting welcome for Kate Greenaway, and the one that she herself would most have loved.

BEATRIX POTTER

Beatrix potter was surely the most modest of author-illustrators. When a friend showed her an admiring article about her work, Beatrix scoffed at it. "Great rubbish!" she said. "Absolute bosh!" In later life, she preferred to think of herself as a sheep farmer rather than a writer.

Yet she took pride in her writing and art and was a perfectionist in both. In her narrative, every word is precisely chosen. The descriptions are pointed, the dialogue flavorful, the characters sharply observed.

Her drawings and exquisite water colors are executed with the same loving care. Beatrix once showed an American visitor a portfolio of fungi drawings, explaining that she had studied fungi intensively for years and had filled seven portfolios with drawings. But she was still not satisfied. "It needed a scientist," she said.

A child of the Victorian age, Beatrix Potter was born in Kensington, in central London, on July 28, 1866. Children were "seen but not heard" in those days. Beatrix and her younger brother, Bertram, lived in the top-floor nurseries of a tall house in Bolton Gardens. They were fortunate in the kindly nurse and governess who brought them up, because their remote parents led a social life. With Beatrix they were strict and discouraging. When the artist, John Millais, a family friend, offered to paint their plump little daughter, the offer was refused. It might make her vain!

Beatrix and Bertram enjoyed each other's company and shared hobbies which clearly showed the direction their talents were taking. They loved animals, liked to draw and paint, and delighted in making tiny, handsewn books which they filled with pictures.

For city children, they had a surprising variety of pets. Not only the kitchen tabby but mice, minnows, hedgehogs, rabbits and even an owl, smuggled home from vacations in Wales, Scotland, and the Lake District, to which Beatrix lost her heart. "My brother and I were born in London," she wrote once, "but our descent, our interests and joy were all in the north country."

Bertram was packed off to Charterhouse, a fine old boarding school, but Beatrix was educated at home. "I am glad I did not go to school," she said. "It would have rubbed off some of the originality (if I had not died of shyness) . . . ." She was permitted a few drawing lessons, and Millais showed her how to mix her paints. But for the most part she went her own way. "Painting cannot be taught," she said flatly.

Although a lonely girl, Beatrix was never unhappy nor bored. She spent much of her time in the Museum of Practical Geology and the Natural History and Science Museums of South Kensington, copying exhibits. A sensitive observer, before long she became selective, producing individual and charming pictures which were also scientifically accurate.

There was plenty to see in the streets of Kensington. Rich and poor mingled in the neighborhood, where great houses rubbed shoulders with streets of little cottages, tiny general stores, and blacksmiths' forges. From her high window, Beatrix could spot anyone from an elegant coachman to a "Blue Coat boy," an orphan from the famous Christ's Hospital, archaic in long blue coat, white neckband, highly polished black shoes, and bright yellow stockings.

At fifteen, Beatrix began a journal, using a code which she invented herself. Like the Brontës before her, she wrote in a minute script, and it was years after her death before Leslie Linder, an admirer of her work, broke the code and deciphered the mass of material.

She continued the journal until she was thirty, filling it with observations, art criticism, opinions, and wryly humorous accounts of her daily doings. Of a visit to the dentist, she said: "He did not hurt me in the least, only he had only just come in when *we* did, and his fingers tasted muchly of kid gloves."

Beatrix Potter's first published work was a set of colored pictures, an experiment in illustrating. She also did a series of line drawings for *Uncle Remus*. But she decided against illustrating as a career. "Illustrators soon begin to go downhill," she wrote to her publisher, "I will stick to doing as many as I can of my own books."

Her first book, and several others, were derived from picture-letters. She wrote many of these engaging letters, usually to the children of Mrs. Moore, her former governess. "I don't know what to write to you, so I shall tell you a story about four little rabbits, whose names were Flopsy, Mopsy, Cottontail and Peter," the letter began. Years later, when she was thirty-six, she added more pictures and submitted it to a publisher, Frederick Warne. He rejected it, but Beatrix believed in it and had it printed at her own expense. Its modest success made Frederick Warne reconsider. Beatrix revised the story for him, gave it colored illustrations, and in 1902 Peter Rabbit made his formal bow in *The Tale of Peter Rabbit*. He soon became the darling of small readers from Calcutta to Kalamazoo.

Beatrix found mice the most endearing of creatures and loved to observe their shy antics. So her next book, *The Tailor of Gloucester,* was a "mouse book," based on a picture-letter written to Freda Moore. During a visit to the Cotswolds, a hill district of old-world beauty, Beatrix had heard a tale about a tailor who came to his shop one morning to find his work finished for him—except for one sleeve, to which was pinned a laconic note, "No more twist." Retelling the story, Beatrix illustrated it with beguiling pictures, including a splendid one of Simpkin, the mouse-tailor's cat, stalking through the snow. The picture proved unforgettable. In 1958, when author Joan Bodger and her family made a literary pilgrimage to England, they stopped their car in front of College Court, the house where the tailor had rented a kitchen. Nearby, under an arch, they glimpsed "a haughty tortoiseshell cat, shaking rain water from his paws in such a disgusted and Simpkin-like manner that it seemed impossible for him to be other."

More picture-letters, and more books, followed, always concerned with animals, flowers, and landscape. Human beings seldom appeared in them, for Beatrix was not successful in drawing people. In *The Tale of Squirrel Nutkin,* 1903, she turned to the squirrels which appeared mysteriously on a Lakeland island the moment the nuts were ripe. *The Tale of Benjamin Bunny* followed in 1904. A sequel to *Peter Rabbit,* it is told with humor and relish and contains some of her best drawings.

Beatrix Potter was especially successful in drawing these miniature worlds which children love. In *The Tale of Two Bad Mice,* 1904, Tom Thumb and Hunca Munca, drawn from life, inhabit a mousehole and a dollhouse. Small children are captivated by this tale. In *Books Before Five,* Dorothy White tells of a little girl who, hearing it for the first time, cried, "I love it, I love it. Again!"

In 1905, when she was thirty-nine, Beatrix became engaged to Norman Warne, youngest member of the publishing firm, a gentle, understanding man with whom she discussed every detail of her books. In spite of her parents' opposition, the pair would have married, but Norman died suddenly before the end of the year.

Up to this time, Beatrix had been a dutiful daughter, living with her parents in the spinster fashion of the day. But now she made a move which startled them. With the money from her books, and a small legacy, she bought Hill Top Farm, in Sawrey, a village in her beloved Lake District. She allowed the tenant to remain as overseer but she stayed at the farm whenever she could for as long as she could. Biographer Marcus Crouch tells of her "supervising improvements to the buildings, battling with workmen, watching the growth of stock, energetically exterminating rats." Unusual for an artist, she proved an astute businesswoman, buying up tracts of land around the farm until she eventually owned most of the village.

During the next eight years, she published twelve more books, with Sawrey and Hill Top Farm as the inspiration for whimsical plots and lively pictures. The landscape in *The Tale of Jemima Puddleduck,* 1908, "is of her best," says Marcus Crouch, "particularly the scenes when Jemima sets off over the hill in search of a safe place, free of 'superflous hens,' for her nest."

To please young readers who were clamoring for more about Peter Rabbit, she wrote *The Tale of the Flopsy Bunnies,* 1909, using her uncle's Welsh home as background. On page fourteen, there is a delightful touch, a sign advertising the rabbits' specialties: PETER RABBIT AND MOTHER—FLORISTS —GARDENS NEATLY RAZED. BORDERS DEVASTATED BY THE NIGHT OR YEAR.

In Sawrey, Beatrix had engaged a country lawyer, William Heelix, to look after her interests. A gentle man with a quiet sense of humor, his deep feeling for the land matched her own. Belonging to the Lake District, he was able to tell Beatrix much about its old farms, its farmers, and shepherds. Soon they were enjoying long walks together and finding each other compatible. When, in 1913, William asked her to marry him, Beatrix accepted readily, although her parents again raised objections.

Free at last to live where she wished, she moved into her husband's home, Castle Cottage, just up the lane from Hill Top Farm. But she kept her own hideaway as it was. When author Anne Carroll Moore visited her in 1921, Beatrix allowed her to explore Hill Top Farm. The American found it "exactly as it was pictured in *The Roly-Poly Pudding*— the kitchen chimney up which Tom Kitten jumped, the cupboard where Moppet and Mittens were shut, the staircase on which Mrs. Twitchit pattered up and down . . . the mysterious attic where Ribby and Tabitha heard the roly-poly noise."

While children continued to revel in her books and beg for more, Beatrix withdrew from her imaginary world to grapple with the realities of farming life. Her energies went into caring for her farm and livestock, and into the breeding of pedigreed Herdwick sheep. It was what she wanted to do.

Although, at her publisher's urging, she wrote a few more books, they were generally based on early picture-letters and contained nothing very new. *Appley Dapply's Nursery Rhymes,* 1917, and *Cecily Parsley's Nursery Rhymes,* 1922, are written with her special brand of humor and illustrated with some of her finest drawings. *The Fairy Caravan,* 1929, and *The Tale of the Faithful Dove,* written in 1907 but not published until 1955, are the least successful of her works.

With her husband's counsel, she continued to add to her land. Canon Rawnsley, Vicar of Wray, one of her few old friends, had aroused her interest in England's National Trust, which acquires land and houses of natural beauty and interest to ensure their preservation. Deciding to do all she could to preserve the beauty and character of the Lake District, Beatrix bought some thousands of acres, which she donated to the Trust.

Best of all for lovers of her books, she bequeathed Hill Top Farm to the nation, not as a personal shrine but as an example of a typical Lakeland farm.

Although the evils of the Second World War grieved her deeply, Beatrix never lost her spirit or her humor. "Let us hope for peace before another New Year," she wrote in a letter of 1940. "But we will just stick it out, whatever happens. . . . People take it calmly, with temper, not fear. The sheep and cattle take no notice."

Beatrix Potter died at the age of seventy-seven, on December 22, 1943. Her books continue to be widely reprinted; *The Journal of Beatrix Potter,* first published in 1966, is be-

ginning to be known. And in the beautiful reproductions of
her drawings and water colors in *The Art of Beatrix Potter*,
we can trace the development of an artist "who went straight
to the natural world for inspiration and to children for an
appreciation of her art."

ROBERT LAWSON

To win either the Caldecott or the Newbery Award is a great honor for an author or illustrator. To win both is a rare achievement. Robert Lawson, the distinguished author-illustrator is, to date, the only person to have done so.

Robert Lawson was born in New York City on September 4, 1892. His family moved to Montclair, New Jersey, an old and pleasant town with fine libraries, private and public art galleries, and a world-famous iris garden. Here the young Robert spent a happy and orderly suburban childhood.

Unlike most illustrators, he showed no precocious talent for drawing or painting. It was not until his high-school years that he began to take an interest in art, possibly generated by visits to the small but significant Montclair Art Museum, which has frequent shows of the work of contemporary and other artists.

After graduating from Montclair High School, he attended the New York School of Fine and Applied Art, where he studied illustrating under Howard Giles. Mingling with art students, he inevitably found his way to Greenwich Village, the writers' and artists' quarter of New York City.

In 1914, he took a studio in the Village where, for three years, he did magazine work, stage settings, and commercial art. Unlike other beginning artists, he did not despise such work, nor was he impatient with its demands. He realized that it gave him invaluable experience in a number of media and was also excellent discipline.

In 1917, shortly after America entered World War One, Robert Lawson went to France to serve in the Camouflage Section of the 40th Engineers. His experience in scene painting stood him in good stead as he did camouflage work at the Front.

Camouflage (the word comes from the French *camoufler*, to blind or veil) is a very old principle of deceiving the enemy by artificial aids. The appearance of troops, trenches, or fortifications was altered so as to make them invisible or assimilate them into the surrounding countryside. So important did camouflage become with the growth of air power that guns, tanks, vehicles, and buildings of all kinds were painted in such a way as to deceive the observer from the air. He also taught it in the artillery schools.

Returning home at the war's end, Robert Lawson received his first commission from W. Martin Johnson, then the art editor of *Delineator* and *Designer*. For some years, he worked exclusively for those two magazines, developing a style of his own and learning much from their highly capable editor. Among others, he illustrated a long fairy story by George Randolph Chester and the *Rootabaga Stories* of Carl Sandburg. These modern tales, filled with fantasy and airy nonsense, appealed to him strongly.

In 1922, he married Marie Abrams, a native of Georgia, herself a writer and illustrator of charming books for children. A woman of many resources, indoors and out, she proved a stimulating companion. During her girlhood, her father had taught her to ride horseback, and she had explored the then wilderness country of North Carolina. Now she and Robert sailed together on Long Island Sound and spent their vacations in Nantucket, an island south of Cape Cod, which retains its old atmosphere and the distinctive physical character which it inherited from years of Quaker dominance and whaling prosperity.

In 1923, the Lawsons built a home in Westport, Connecticut, which they named "Rabbit Hill." "It really is a hill and there really are rabbits," wrote Helen Fish, in a biographical sketch of Lawson. "The studio looks out over a field of them and sometimes he finds them in the hillside garden." "Rabbit Hill" was dear to the Lawsons, although Mrs. Lawson once observed, "I am very happy at 'Rabbit Hill,' save for an unreasonable wish that blue water, instead of meadow land, lay beyond our pine trees."

For some years, husband and wife shared a studio, producing magazine illustrations and commercial art, "as well," said Robert, "as turning out huge numbers of greeting cards." But by 1930, with the Depression under way, this source of income dried up.

In that same year, he was given his first book to illustrate, Arthur Mason's *Wee Men of Ballywooden*. He later illustrated other of Mason's books, and his preoccupation with delicate pen and ink work led him to etching. In 1931, he won the John Taylor Arms Prize, awarded annually by the Society of American Etchers. He also gave his first one-man show, about which one critic commented, "No definite story is ever told in Robert Lawson's etchings. There is no beginning and no end, but for the space of a breath a door swings ajar into another world and those who choose may enter in." His wife also paid tribute to this "other world" quality of

Lawson's work. "His special world is really this world of our own," she said once, "amplified and enriched by a wider horizon. Within it, because of his singularly vivid awareness, figures of history move out not as ghosts but as living men and women, fields and forest are still peopled by those fantastic beings who never existed save in the imagination of men throughout the ages."

After 1930, he began to do more and more book illustrating and less commercial art. The books he chose to illustrate were very varied; among them were Margarey Bianco's *Hurdy-Gurdy Man,* Elizabeth Coatsworth's *Golden Horseshoe,* a book of old nursery rhymes called *Four and Twenty Blackbirds,* and Eleanor Farjeon's *One Foot in Fairyland.* One of the most important books he illustrated was Bunyan's *Pilgrim's Progress,* in which the drawings reach the stature of his finest etchings.

After 1935, seeking a new and special medium, he developed a brush-and-black-tempera method of his own, which was a rubbed or brushed Woolf pencil technique on smooth Whatman drawing board. "The whole process consists of an endless series of drawing, brushing, picking out lights with the rubber, and then doing it over and over again, finally fixing and picking out the highlights with white tempera or by scraping with a knife," he explained in an article in *Art Instruction.*

This method reached perfection in Lawson's illustrations for Munro Leaf's *The Story of Ferdinand,* the perennial favorite about a young bull who would rather smell the flowers than fight.

In 1939, he wrote and illustrated his own first book, *Ben and Me.* A fine example of biographical fiction, it is a hilarious story of Benjamin Franklin, as told by his mouse, Amos. The facts of Franklin's life are accurate, but Amos takes the credit for most of his master's accomplishments. The illustrations are richly humorous.

In 1941, Lawson was awarded the Caldecott Medal for *They Were Strong and Good,* an unusual book with striking full-page illustrations of his pioneer forbears and their surroundings and doings in the United States. The simple text inspires pride of ancestry and love of country in its young readers, for it "is not alone the story of my parents and grandparents," Lawson says in his foreword, "it is the story of the parents and grandparents of most of us who call ourselves Americans."

In 1945, Robert Lawson won the Newbery Award with *Rabbit Hill,* a gentle, happy story about the animals living on his own grounds. As the tale opens, the little creatures are worrying about the New Folks who have bought Rabbit Hill. Previous tenants had let the grounds run down. Would the New Folks be an improvement—or would they be worse?

Porky the Woodchuck soon brings reassuring news. "Everybody says they're planting folks, Mole," he cries, "and maybe there'll be seed again in the tool-shed, seeds and chicken feed. And it'll fall through the cracks and we'll have all we can eat all winter. And there'll be heat in the cellar and we can build burrows right against the wall and be warm and cosy again."

The New Folks arrive and are put on probation. But they prove themselves; they rescue Little Willie, the fieldmouse, from drowning in a rain barrel, and they nurse Little George, the rabbit, after his car accident. Best of all, they put up a large sign saying PLEASE DRIVE CAREFULLY ON AC-COUNT OF SMALL ANIMALS. How the animals learn to trust the New Folks, and how they repay their kindnesses—all this makes a tender little story. The beautifully detailed illustrations are in black and white.

The Tough Winter, 1954, is a sequel to *Rabbit Hill,* with the same animal characters and the same faultless combination of text and pictures. When the Folks go away for the winter, the caretaker and his mean dog make life hard for the animals, who are near starvation. Uncle Analdas, "the old, old rabbit," helps by foraging and eventually succeeds in bringing the folk home from the Bluegrass country. Then everyone is happy again. "All traces of the ice storm's damage had been cleaned up. . . . Shrubs, lawns and gardens, protected and nourished by the winter-long blanket of snow, were more lush than usual. The Animals too had resumed their sleek, well-fed appearance. Uncle Analdas's left ear, slightly frost-bitten, was a bit more disreputable-looking than formerly. Otherwise no one showed any effect of the recent hard times."

Robert Lawson achieved some of his most effective writing when he put animals into close relationship with human beings. In *Mr. Revere and I,* 1953, the events that produced the Minute Men during the American Revolution are related by Paul Revere's horse. Sherry. This form of narration lends itself to considerable wry humor. Sold to "Stinky Nat," the proprietor of a glue factory, Sherry observes, "Of course this rude bumpkin was no horseman; I could have tossed him off as easily as a sack of grain. But naturally, for a horse of my breeding, this would never do. For one must never, never allow one's personal feelings to interfere in the perfor-

mance of one's horsely duties. Ajax expressed this so splendidly when he used to say 'After all my dear, like 'im or not,
your master is your master.' "

Whether he was busy with commercial art, illustrating the
books of others, or writing and illustrating his own books,
Robert Lawson showed unfailing integrity. Even during his
commercial period, nothing was ever hastily conceived, nothing was skimped. "Each job added something to his stature
as an artist," said Helen Fish. As an illustrator he met the
challenge of fine texts and enriched lesser ones with his
imaginative drawings. And his own books, with their appealing subjects, their humor and tenderness, are a joy forever to
juvenile book lovers of all ages.

WANDA GAG

When, at four, Wanda Gág went to her first school, she was enchanted with all the things she was given to work with—beads and straws, sewing cards, strands of colored wool, pastel-tinted papers. What wonders she would create with such riches!

If she were alive now, Wanda would be delighted to know that today's teachers find her *Nothing At All* ideal for "telling with a felt board." In this medium, which Wanda would have loved as a child, flannel-backed illustrations are placed on a felt-covered board to be gazed at by small listeners as the story unfolds. Other pictures are added as the tale moves along. "In what other way could Gág's Nothing At All complete his metamorphosis from a round ball, to the shape of a dog, to a live dog with spots, ears and tail that wags?" asks educator Charlotte S. Huck.

Wanda Gág had a peculiar talent for combining text and pictures in an unforgettable way. Her *Millions of Cats* is sometimes called "the first American picture book." Certainly one of the earliest, it is still one of the best. Story and pictures seem to flow together, as her gnomelike old man traipses over hill and dale to the refrain of "millions and billions and trillions of cats."

Gág stories are perfect for reading aloud. They get off to a

quick start. "Once upon a time there were three little orphan dogs. They were brothers. They lived in a far forgotten
corner of an old forgotten farm in three forgotten kennels
which stood there in a row." There is plenty of action, an
exciting climax, natural conversation, and the happy ending
which children demand. Perhaps because of her Bohemian
ancestry, her stories have the feeling of folk tales; like folk
tales, they have been polished and repolished by loving repe-
tition.

Wanda Gág was born on March 11, 1893, in New Ulm,
Minnesota. The trim little town had been settled by Middle
Europeans like Wanda's grandparents, all four of whom had
come from Bohemia. Residents of New Ulm kept up their
old-world customs; they told Bavarian and Bohemian legends and folk tales, and took part in German marches and
athletics. German-speaking Wanda did not know a word of
English until she started school.

Her father, Anton Gág, was a talented artist, frustrated in
his ambition to study art in Europe, or at least under good
masters. With a wife and seven children to provide for, he
earned a living by painting and decorating houses. Sunday
was reserved for his own pictures. "On Sundays my father
was happy in his soul," Wanda wrote once.

Wanda's mother, Lissi, was a tiny woman, tender, kind,
and charmingly creative where her children were concerned.
She dressed her five daughters in soft, free-flowing clothes instead of in the constricting fashions of the day. She designed
fanciful costumes for their play-acting, turned the garden
into a playground, improvised stories, and dreamed up little
surprises. "When she baked bread, she always made little
square *Bilder-Bucher* (picture books), which were pieces of

45

dough cut into small pieces," says Wanda's friend and biographer, Alma Scott. "After these were nicely browned in the oven, the children opened them, spread butter inside, and literally devoured the books."

The Gág home, with its turrets and gables and round, two-storied porch, was just right for imaginative children. Inside, it was different from the houses around. Anton himself had painted the dining-room ceiling as a blue sky, with cherubs tumbling from drifting clouds. The third floor, reached by a trap door, was a magic land of attics. One was a playroom; one was crammed with shelves of art books and with Anton's collection of Indian costumes and regalia.

Most awesome was the long middle attic, Anton's studio, complete with skylight and sloping roof. Here, as a very small child, Wanda would sit in silence, watching her father at his easel.

From an early age, all the Gág children drew. Anton criticized their work in all seriousness. "Tracing was taboo. Copying other people's work was frowned upon," says Alma Scott. "Instead, the children were encouraged to draw the things which they remembered or imagined and, as soon as they seemed ready, to draw from life or from actual objects around them."

For Wanda, childhood came to an end with the death of her father. With his dying words, Anton shaped his daughter's future. "What Papa couldn't do, Wanda will have to finish," he said. He wanted her to become an artist, and that was what she wanted for herself.

Life became a struggle for the Gágs. Later, Wanda was to write: "Besides our home, there was left to us some twelve hundred dollars insurance money which, with the addition of eight dollars a month from the county, was made to stretch over the next six years."

Critical neighbors distressed the fifteen-year-old Wanda with tart suggestions that she leave school and get a job as a clerk. But Wanda and Lissi were determined that all the children should have at least a high-school education and that Wanda, as soon as practicable, should have formal art lessons.

Although it went against the grain, Wanda turned at once to the kind of "art" that would bring in a few dollars to help the family. She drew postcards and place cards, made calendars, and wrote and illustrated stories and poems which won cash prizes in the children's pages of the *Minneapolis Journal.*

After attending high school half time, Wanda graduated in 1912. While considering what to do, she continued to draw salable trifles. But she never forgot her real objective; in the time left from housework and child care, she applied herself seriously to her art, "trying to work more true to life, with expression and strong, bold lines." To her gratification, a sketch of her sister Stella, which she entered in a contest run by the St. Paul Institute of Arts, won a bronze medal as the second-best entry in the state. It also brought a favorable criticism of her work and the suggestion that she begin formal study as soon as possible.

The St. Paul Institute offered Wanda free tuition for a year, an offer she had to refuse because she could not afford to live away from home. Deciding to teach school while the children—Stella, Tussy, Asta, Dehli, Howard, and Flavia— were getting an education, she took the necessary examinations for her certificate and, in the fall of the year, obtained

47

a position in a rural school.

She proved a spirited and innovative teacher. The children loved her for her gaiety and beauty, and Wanda, in turn, liked teaching and country life. She was made much of in the community, especially by the young men.

After the summer vacation, she had an irresistible offer. Charles Weschcke, a former resident of New Ulm and an admirer of Anton Gág's work, proposed to finance her so that she could take advantage of the year of free tuition offered by the St. Paul Institute. Assured by the family that they would manage to get along without her, Wanda accepted eagerly. "A crash will have to come," she wrote to Alma, "such joy can't last—can it?"

Art school proved a mixed blessing. Cherishing her individualism and originality, Wanda did not always agree with her teachers. She objected to spending so much time drawing from casts. In class, she often dreamed rather than drew, and she seldom handed in assignments.

Life outside the school was more productive, and happier. In her room at the YWCA she worked constantly. When the Chicago Grand Opera Company came to town, she got permission to sketch the singers in their exotic costumes; they were amazed at how well she caught their likenesses.

With Alma, she explored the city during long rambles. She found escorts eager to take her to concerts, the opera, theaters. Best of all, she had a friend and confidant in Armand Emraad, a young medical student who was enthusiastic about her work. She even had a number of proposals but, at that stage of her career, she feared that marriage would be difficult to reconcile with art.

She did not return to St. Paul after her year was up. After

a vacation at home, she took a job in commercial art. But the work was grueling, a strain on her health and eyesight. She was rescued by Herschel V. Jones, managing editor of the *Minneapolis Journal,* who had been shown some of her sketches. The *Journal* offered her free instruction at the Minneapolis School of Art, plus an allowance for her living expenses. Although warned that she would find the teaching every bit as conventional as that in St. Paul, Wanda accepted gratefully.

History repeated itself. Wanda acted and reacted to her teachers just as she had done in St. Paul. Nevertheless, the experience was profitable. When the school moved to the handsome new Minneapolis Institute of Arts, she was able to do something wholly new to her—study actual masterpieces of painting and sculpture.

During her second year in Minneapolis, she turned reluctantly to advertising art, made pastel portraits at a dollar apiece, and sold sketches to the newspapers. She despised such "slick" art, but it enabled her to send money home. "Dear God," she wrote in her diary, "suffer me to fight all my life, all my life; but do not let me stop at being a clever illustrator."

Early in the following year, she was called home. Her mother was ill, and Wanda was needed. Stella and Tussy, both away teaching, sent home what money they could, but there was never enough for pressing needs, "for food and fuel and clothing, let alone for taxes, for repairs that had to be made on the old house, for sidewalks that must be laid, for dentist's and doctor's bills."

In sub-zero weather, while the family was snowbound, Lissi Gág died, leaving Wanda to care for teen-aged Asta, and the youngsters, Dehli, Howard, and Flavia.

The following April, Wanda heard that she had been awarded a scholarship to study at the New York Art Students' League. A family council was held, at which it was decided to sell the house and move to Minneapolis. But buyers were slow in coming. While they waited, Wanda was commissioned to illustrate *A Child's Book of Folklore*. When it was finished, she headed for New York. Meanwhile, Stella and Tussy had found jobs in Minneapolis, where the others would eventually join them.

Wanda found New York City stimulating and the teaching at the Art Students League after her own heart. At last she met artist-instructors like Rockwell Kent and C. Lewis Hind who "preached the very freedom and individuality for which she had been striving."

When the house was finally sold, the Gágs were reunited in an apartment in Minneapolis. With Stella and Tussy working, Asta posing for art students, Howard earning seven dollars a week, and the youngest girls in school, Wanda felt free to continue living in New York. Not for further study, except on her own, but to do freelance work.

For a time, she shared a walk-up apartment with two other artists, doing anything she could to make a living. She painted lampshades, did batik work, even created a few toys. Before many years passed, she found that she could earn a substantial living in fashion designing—and she faced a familiar problem. Should she continue with commercial art and its prosperity? Or should she give it up entirely, retire to the country, and devote herself to the serious art she loved? She was free to choose: Stella and Asta were married now, Tussy was in New York, and the younger Gágs had finished school and were able to look after themselves.

Wanda decided on pure art. She spent her savings on an unpretentious cottage in Ridgefield, Connecticut, where she was exquisitely happy. "Everything seemed to say to her, 'Why not draw me? . . . . I'm an old house, see my noble crooked lines—I'm a hillside, I unfold myself to you as a symphony. I'll never look like this again—better capture me now!' "

In 1926, Wanda held her first exhibition at the Weyhe Gallery in New York City. Critics as far away as Denver, Colorado, acclaimed the striking realism of her work. Murdock Pemberton wrote in *The New Yorker:* "We have seen no lithographs or drawings we liked as much since the show of Matisse, two years ago."

Wanda moved to another home, an old, rugged, very paintable little house in New Jersey, which she named "Tumble Timbers." Here, for the next few years, she was enormously productive, making lithographs, linoleum cuts, wood engravings, sketches, paintings, and drawings. Her second showing at the Weyhe Gallery established her reputation. She had splendidly fulfilled her father's ambition for her, and her own.

The year 1930 brought a new home, and a husband, Earl Humpheys, an unusual and non-mercenary businessman. The pair lost their hearts to a 100-year-old home in the Muscanetcong Mountain region of New Jersey. This they made into a charming, commodious home, spacious enough for work and visitors. Wanda, because of the possibilities of its 125 acres, named it "All Creation."

Impressed by the pictures in Wanda's second exhibit, Evangeline Evans, an editor in the publishing firm of Coward, McCann, asked her whether she would care to illustrate a children's book. Wanda replied by showing her an unfinished story, *Millions of Cats*. Miss Evans pounced on it delightedly and at once contracted for Wanda to finish the book and illustrate it herself.

Published in 1928, *Millions of Cats* was immediately successful. It has since been printed in Braille, and translated into many languages. To fill a demand for more Gág books, Wanda wrote *The Funny Thing*, 1929, and *Snippy and Snappy*, 1931. Both stories had been brewing for years and were now written and illustrated with scrupulous care. "I aim to make the illustrations for children's books as much a work of art as anything I would send to an art exhibition," Wanda said. And that aim was beautifully realized.

Her next book, *The ABC Bunny,* was illustrated with lithographs in velvety blacks and grays. The bunny rambles through fields and gardens, having happy encounters with porcupines and squirrels, owls and quail. Small children love the merry verse that follows Bunny's adventures.

One of her more unusual undertakings was the translation and illustration of some fifty of Grimm's fairy tales, a project at which she worked, off and on, for several years. Between times, she produced two more of her own books, *Nothing at All*, 1941, and *Gone Is Gone*, 1935, an endearingly comical tale of "the man who wanted to do his wife's housework."

At the request of her publishers, Wanda also brought out *Growing Pains,* a nostalgic selection of entries from her early diaries. "Since its publication in 1940," says Alma Scott, *"Growing Pains* has become recognized as a classic picture of the adolescent years. Teenage readers find in it a reflection of their own problems and wonderings, and it brought

Wanda much fan mail from high school girls and young people who also wanted to be artists."

In January, 1945, Wanda's health began to fail, and in February lung cancer was diagnosed. Yet, in the seventeen months remaining to her, she never lost interest in her work. When she felt strong enough to draw, she drew. When she was too weak to hold a pencil, she mulled over fairy tales or reminiscences of her childhood in New Ulm.

She died at All Creation on June 27, 1946. The drawings and fairy tales on which she had worked during her illness were published as *More Tales from Grimm*. They were prepared with the same loving and scrupulous care she had given to all her books and illustrations.

"Anton Gág would have been proud," writes Alma Scott. "Those last drawings, some of them unfinished, give mute testimony to the fact that she kept steadily on until the last; their humor, irrepressible still, tells that her spirit was unconquerable to the end."

LOIS LENSKI

In a biographical sketch of author-illustrator Lois Lenski, Maud Hart Lovelace describes her as being "as American as Plymouth Rock." This she is, in spite of a grandfather born in Poland and a grandmother born in Russia. One of the best American authors of regional stories, she has explored many regions of the United States, each very different from the other; she has joined in the life of the people, listened to their experiences, eaten their food, and made detailed sketches of their homes and furnishings. All this fresh, first-hand material she has incorporated into books of warmth and percipience, books like *Strawberry Girl,* a tale of the Florida Crackers; *Bayou Suzette,* which deals with the French-speaking people of Louisiana; and *Blue Ridge Billy,* a tale of the mountain folk of North Carolina.

Besides writing about the contemporary scene, she has brought the American past to life in a number of exciting historical books. *Puritan Adventure* gives a many-sided picture of Puritan life in the Massachusetts Bay Colony. *Indian Captive* tells the true story of Mary Jemison, a young girl who was captured by the Seneca Indians, whom she learned to love and appreciate. Her story, an eye-opener for young readers, shows the Indian character and temperament as they really are, as opposed to the arrant nonsense of the "cowboys and Indians" tales once so readily devoured by children.

Lois Lenski also writes understandingly for the very young, scaling down her plots, pictures, and formats and dealing simply with the mechanics of things which delight small children—sail boats, fire engines, automobiles, and the like. The sum total of her books for all ages adds up to a rounded picture of America and her people, present and past.

Daughter of a Lutheran minister, this unusually prolific author-illustrator was born on October 14, 1893, in Springfield, Ohio. The fourth of five children, she spent her childhood and early teens in the little farming town of Anna, Ohio.

Discipline in the Lenski home was strict and the children were not spoiled, as they often are today, with too many toys, too much entertainment, and too many planned projects. They had to rely on their imagination and make their own fun, and life was the better for it. They had the outdoors for their playground, wild creatures to tame, fruit and berries to pick, trees to climb, and ponds to fish in. Today the adult Lois Lenski still gardens, raises her own vegetables, and bottles her home-grown fruit.

While still very young, Lois loved to draw but had no idea of how to compose her own pictures. Painstakingly, she copied the bright covers of magazines or traced flowers from seed catalogs. Her parents, though each loved beauty, had little knowledge or awareness of art and saw no particular significance in their child's absorption in drawing. But a commercial fresco painter, who came to Anna to decorate the church, understood her need and suggested that she be given a box of paints.

At least two of her teachers were more perceptive than her parents. During her senior year in high school, her English teacher recognized that Lois had a gift for writing. "I feel sure that you will do some kind of creative work," she wrote to her after graduation. She suggested that Lois make English her major in college.

Lois, however, was still preoccupied with drawing. When the family moved to Columbus, she entered Ohio State University, majored in art, and took her B.S. in education. She had intended to teach, but one of her art teachers advised her to study for a year at the Art Students League in New York City.

Her father found the idea incredible. He wanted his daughter to teach. Teaching was a respected profession, and spelled security. He had already paid for her college training and would certainly not pay further expenses so that she could waste her time in New York City!

Undeterred, Louis took her own small savings—and "the sleeper" to New York. For the next four years, she studied part time at the Art Students League, enjoying every minute of it. To support herself, she did odd jobs, usually in some form of commercial art. Like Wanda Gág, she painted place cards and Christmas cards but, unlike Wanda, she did it without resentment, perhaps realizing that the work was a useful steppingstone. "Whenever I was allowed to choose my own subject, I drew children," she told Maud Hart Lovelace. "I never consciously made up my mind to be a 'children's author or artist' or to work exclusively for them. It was all a gradual growth, unconsciously pointing in one direction."

In 1920, she went to England, where she studied for a year

at the Westminster School of Art in London. While there, she illustrated her first books, notably one by Kenneth Grahame, author of the classic *The Wind in the Willows*.

She returned home at a good moment. The publishing houses, which had been hard hit during World War One, were active again. Illustrators were needed, and she had no trouble in getting commissions. For Minton, Balch and Company, she illustrated the *Chimney Corner* anthologies, catching their spirit of fantasy in her stylized trees and flowers, her gentle colors and curved border designs.

In 1921, she married a widower, Arthur Covey, and achieved a ready-made family, a stepdaughter of twelve and a stepson of four. Her husband was a mural painter of note, and the pair were compatible, each respecting the other's needs and each working serenely in his own studio. When their son, Stephen, was born, the little family was complete, with enough children to serve Lois as an audience for her books.

She continued to illustrate the work of contemporary authors, who found her scrupulously attentive to their needs and wishes. To date, Lois Lenski has illustrated some fifty-seven books by others and about a hundred of her own. A formidable number, but her interest has never flagged and each book has been given its own original character.

Her first book, *Skipping Village,* was published in 1927 and was followed, in 1928, by *A Little Girl of 1900.* Based on childhood experiences, they recreate the people, activities, and atmosphere of a lovable small town, much like the one in which Lois grew up.

When her son Stephen was small, she struck a rich vein of material while watching him and his friends. They were, she says, "constantly playing at 'auto.' Tricycle, wagon or kiddie-car was always an imaginary auto. They were always pumping up tires, putting in gas and water, and getting stuck in the mud."

The result of her observations was a happy outpouring of picture books, starting with *The Little Family* in 1932. In 1934 came *The Little Auto,* which introduced "the versatile Mr. Small." Dapper in his bowler hat and red bow tie, Mr. Small goes for a ride in his auto, scaring ducks and chickens, but obeying the traffic laws. He gets caught in a downpour and has a flat tire. But Mr. Small is smart. He puts on the spare, and soon the little auto is back in its garage. "After it is washed and polished, it shines like new."

Radiating good humor and brisk common sense, Mr. Small appears in book after book. In *The Little Farmer,* he busies himself with the farm machinery. In *Policeman Small* he is a traffic cop. "Oh, do you know Policeman Small?" asks the song which precedes his story:

> He is the nicest friend of all!
> He tells the cars to stop and go
> Or keeps them waiting in a row.

Although dressed as an adult, Mr. Small is child-sized in the illustrations. Maud Hart Lovelace says, "Many a mother observes how the child reader identifies with Mr. Small; how, after finishing the book, he wants to put on overalls and go out and *be* Mr. Small."

For the pre-school child, Lois Lenski has written the *Davy* books, small in format, with brief text and with pictures that look "right" to the child. To make sure that all is crystal clear, Lois Lenski always makes a dummy of the book, enlisting groups of small readers to comment on it as she proceeds. "Children have kept me from some awful blunders," she told an interviewer. "Once I had a cow standing on a fence and didn't know it. I *thought* she was in the field back of the fence, but her hoof was touching the top rail, and to a child who does not understand perspective it looked as though she were standing on the fence. When I moved the foot one eighth of an inch, the children were satisfied."

A glutton for the work she loves, Lois Lenski eventually overtaxed her strength, and years of writing, illustrating, child care, and domestic chores took their toll. For the sake of her health, she was ordered to winter in the South.

This she did, cheerfully making a virtue of necessity—and the result was a fine new departure in her writing and illustrating. She soon began her most meaningful project, a series of regional books, designed to widen the horizons and sympathies of nine- to fifteen-year-olds. These she illustrated with soft pencil drawings, filled with accurate detail. The pictures of people are wholly human and real.

A sojourn in New Orleans provided the material for *Bayou Suzette,* of which columnist Dorothy Dix said, "It is as full of meat and as flavorsome as good gumbo filé—no better pictures have ever been drawn of Baratavia fishing folk."

Other regional books followed, among them *Cotton in My Sack, Judy's Journey,* and *Strawberry Girl.* Each showed children and a way of life for the most part totally unfamiliar to its young readers. "I am trying to present vivid, sympathetic pictures of the real life of different localities," Lois said in the foreword of *Strawberry Girl.* "We need to know our country better; to know and understand people different from ourselves; so that we can say: 'This then is the way these people live. Because I understand it, I admire and love them.' " Ahead of her time, she was concentrating on a subject which today concerns us all deeply—the underprivileged minorities in our country.

She was ahead of her time, too, in the realism of her writing and her uncompromising choice of characters. People are described precisely as she found them. "She courageously portrays drunken fathers, improvident parents and objectionable neighbors as these are a part of the real life drama of the children in her stories," says Charlotte Huck. But she also shows the redeeming qualities of her characters—family love and loyalty, courage, compassion, and often a natural dignity.

Like Mark Twain, Lois Lenski reproduces the natural speech patterns of her characters, reflecting their regional background and their culture and education—or lack of it. With an educated ear, she reproduces colloquialisms, slang, and vivid turns of speech. In *Strawberry Girl,* when Pa brings Semina, the mule, to the vet, he is told: "Likely her teeth just need filing. . . . Mules grind their food instead of chewing it. Their teeth git very sharp and need to be filed once a year by a mule dentist. . . . No more balkin' now. She'll be as gentle as a cat right on."

Deservedly, the books of Lois Lenski have won a variety of honors. *Indian Captive* was a runner-up for the Newbery Medal in 1942. In 1944 she was awarded the Ohioana Medal for outstanding books written by Ohio authors. *Strawberry Girl* won the Newbery Medal in 1946, and in 1947 *Judy's Journey* carried off the Child Study Association

of America's Children's Book Award for the best book dealing realistically with a contemporary problem. Lois Lenski
has received honorary degrees from the University of North
Carolina and others, while the Catholic Library Association
and the University of Southern Mississippi have honored her
for her past, and continuing, contributions to children's literature.

MARIE HALL ETS

Like Beatrix Potter, Marie Hall Ets writes most often about animals, which she draws with the understanding of a close and loving observer. What is unique is the great variety she presents—animals of the woodlands, the forest, the sea and pond, the farmland, the zoo, the circus, as well as family pets. All are individualized and aptly named—what child could forget Meola, the cat; Cocky, the rooster; Mooloo, the cow; Splop, the goat; or Chukluk, the fat hen?

The media she chooses for her illustrations show unusual diversity and appropriateness. In *Play with Me*, the shadowy pastel sketches capture the mood of awe and wonder as a little girl approaches the shy creatures of woodland and meadow. *Little Old Automobile* and *Mister Penny's Race Horse* rely on black-and-white drawings to give a feeling of movement and a certain folk-tale quality. *Nine Days to Christmas* uses vivid colors to convey the panorama of Mexico and the warmth and jollity of the season.

One of six children, Marie Hall Ets was born in Wisconsin on December 16, 1895, "in a town that got lost" when it merged with the city of Milwaukee. She was a minister's daughter, moving with the family from parsonage to parsonage. The children loved these moves, which never took them too far from the countryside.

The age range of her brothers and sisters was wide, from an elder brother who teased and protected her to a baby whom she was eventually allowed to rock to sleep. "We were shut off in a room by ourselves," she once told her editor, May Massee, "and I hardly dared breathe as I sat at the head of the cradle and rocked. And I was happy for days remembering how he had gone off to sleep the same as he did for the grown-ups." As she grew older, there were nephews and nieces to keep her in close contact with the ways and thoughts of children.

Hers was a carefree childhood. When she wanted to play, there were always boys, girls, and animals to romp with. When she wanted to be alone, the woods were a refuge. Her earliest memories are of family summers in the great North Woods of Wisconsin, where she learned to study and love the wildlife. "I loved to run off by myself into the woods," she says, "and watch for the deer with their fawns, and for porcupines and badgers and turtles and frogs and huge pine snakes and sometimes a bear or a copperhead or a skunk. Later, when old enough to be trusted alone in a flat-bottomed boat, I loved to explore the lakeshore under the low-hanging trees, or the channels between the lakes." Like the little girl in *Play with Me,* she used to sit motionless under the pine trees, waiting for the timid forest creatures to come out of their hiding places.

Few author-illustrators can have started their formal art training as young as she. She was only seven, and in the first grade, when the art supervisor of her school, impressed by her drawing, arranged for her to take instruction with an adult group. They were taught how to copy water colors, usually seascapes. "After that," Marie said amusedly, "I didn't know how to do anything but copy."

Graduating from high school in three years, she entered Lawrence College, where she had a sharp intimation of life's inequities. She herself was sought after by a number of sororities but a friend, a not-too-attractive country girl, was coldly passed over. Stung by this cruelty, Marie refused to join any of the sororities herself. The experience probably had something to do with her later interest in the underprivileged, and the social work which she took up.

After a year in college, she left for more specialized training at the New York School of Fine and Applied Art. In only a year, she gained the two-year diploma in decorating and found herself a job in San Francisco.

Her always active social conscience prompted her to volunteer for work in San Francisco's "Little Italy." While teaching English there she met Milton Rodig, who had just left Stanford University for the army and to whom she soon became engaged. They were married when he was given a two-week furlough, prelude to being shipped out for active service during World War One.

Milton was never to serve. After their short honeymoon, he returned to camp, where he died of pneumonia with shocking suddenness.

In an effort to lose herself in something different, Marie turned from interior decoration to war work. At the Great Lakes Naval Training Station in Waukegan, Illinois, she proved to be well equipped for social work. Her superiors suggested that she take her degrees at the University of Chicago and the School of Civics and Philanthropy. This she did, living in the famous settlement house, Chicago Com-

Edward Lear

Kate Greenaway

Beatrix Potter

Frederick Warne

Viking Press

Robert Lawson

Lois Lenski

Wanda Gág
Coward, McCann & Geoghegan

Marie Hall Ets
Viking Press

H. A. Rey

Houghton Mifflin

Roger Duvoisin

Gunnar Studio

Ludwig Bemelmans

Viking Press, Tony Venti

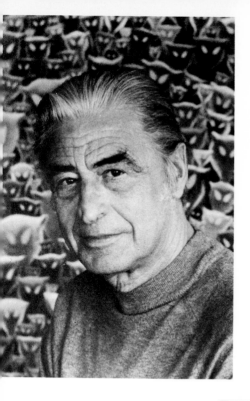

Theodor Geisel (Dr. Seuss)

Leo Lionni

Robert McCloskey

Brinton Turkle

Marcia Brown

Joan Walsh Anglund

Tomi Ungerer

Harper & Row

Maurice Sendak

Harper & Row, Philippe Halsman

Richard Scarry

mons, and doing volunteer duty in whatever time she could spare.

"Of all my volunteer work at the settlement house I think I liked best my classes in toy-making and street games with little children," she told May Massee, perceptive and sympathetic juvenile editor at Viking Press. Marie was not alone in that; at least two other author-illustrators, Maurice Sendak and Marcia Brown, have reveled in creating toys. Probably Marie inherited her creativity from her grandfather who, May Massee writes in a biographical sketch, "was author, doctor, minister, and inventor of the first automobile, made in 1873."

After taking her degrees, she was sent around the country on various projects, one of them being the making of a cost-of-living survey for the United States Coal Commission. This took her into the mountains of West Virginia, where she had to seek out the isolated miner's huts and question the mining families.

Later, she was sent by the Red Cross to Czechoslovakia, where she spent a year organizing a permanent child-health program under the Czech government. Here her social work came to an end; the many experimental shots which she was given to protect her from possible diseases caused her to contract an ailment for which, many years afterward, she still has to undergo treatment.

Returning to the United States, she made her home with a married sister in Wisconsin, where she was accepted delightedly by her little nephews and nieces. During the summer months, the children haunted a nearby farm, made welcome by the farmer and his family. While they played with the animals, their aunt filled her sketchbook. She tells how, one day, as she was drawing the pigs, a young bull charged up behind her and butted her into the brook.

It was probably at this time that she conceived the idea of writing and illustrating picture books. Though she did not realize it, she laid the foundations of her first book when she made an indestructible cloth book, *Little Old Automobile,* for a small nephew who loved to smash his toys.

Returning to her art studies (she continued to study formally throughout her life), Marie took courses for the next few years at the Art Institute of Chicago; at Columbia University; and under Frederick Poole, a member of the Royal Academy of Arts of London, England. In Chicago, she spent much of her leisure time with Harold Ets, a faculty member of the Loyola School of Medicine, whom she had known when she was living in the Chicago Commons. Their friendship ripened and, in spite of her deteriorating health, they decided to marry.

They settled in a delightful house in a woody district on the North Shore of Chicago and Marie soon began to draw the pictures for her first book, *Mister Penny.* "I first tried to do the drawings and tale as children would do them," she says, "but neither Mr. Poole nor May Massee would let me. So after that I didn't try to be anyone but myself." A lovable tale of an old man, the havoc wrought by his frisky pets, and the way they make up for it, the book has bold pictures, full of action and humor.

A volunteer project in which she cooperated with her doctor husband resulted in a unique book in 1939. Loyola University had contributed a remarkable exhibit, showing the growth of the human embryo, to the Chicago Century of

Progress Fair. Dr. Ets, with his wife's assistance, had helped to construct it. From this exhibit she later made large and explicit drawings, which she accompanied with a sensitive and understandable text for small children. "The changing size of the embryo is given reality to the child by continual comparisons with things the child knows—from the size of the tail of a comma (,), to a kernel of rice, to a pussy-willow bud, to a grandmother's thimble," says Ruth R. Irvine in a biographical sketch.

In 1943, Dr. Ets fell ill. While nursing him, his wife worked on *In the Forest,* which was published in 1944. In this beguiling book, a small boy dreams he is walking in the forest. He meets a big lion taking a nap, two brown bears counting their peanuts, two elephant babies taking a bath, and others. Together with the forest animals, the small boy has wonderful games of Hide and Seek and Drop the Hand-kerchief. Text and pictures recreate perfectly the fanciful yet comically practical world of the child's imagination.

After the death of her husband, Marie Hall Ets settled permanently in New York City, although she continued to travel in Alabama, Mexico, and Wisconsin. One summer, she "followed the circuses" in her home state. The experiences resulted in *Mister Penny's Race Horse,* which tells of Mister Penny's dealings with his barnyard friends and Limpy, his horse.

In 1948, the little cloth book which Marie Hall Ets had made for her nephew materialized in a hard cover edition. *Little Old Automobile* has all the ingredients for a successful tale for nursery folk. They recognize their own naughtiness in the automobile's continual "No! I don't want to and I won't!" and follow his rampageous trip with delight. But a sneaking sympathy with the ducks, the gentle cow, and others who have to leap out of the old car's way makes them content to see him meet his Waterloo. Crashing into a train, "Little old automobile never came down again. Just pieces came down."

In spite of continued ill health and the interruptions caused by necessary periods of treatment in Chicago and at the Mayo Clinic in Rochester, Minnesota, Marie Hall Ets has continued to write and illustrate her appealing books, some of which are destined to be nursery classics. *Beasts and Nonsense*, 1952, presents whimsical rhymes, based on zoo animals. *Another Day*, 1953, in gentler vein, is a satisfying sequel to *In the Forest*, in which the elephant, the bears, and others each show what they can do best.

Play with Me, 1955, the most realistic of the Ets' picture books, shows the woodland animals as they are, without humanizing them or fantasizing about them. The little girl in the story realizes that the animals in the wood are afraid of her. She is deeply content when, because of her gentle, patient approach, they begin to respond to her overtures. The pastel illustrations, used here for the first time, are subtle and exquisite.

The crown of the author-illustrator's career came in 1960 when she won the Caldecott Award for *Nine Days to Christmas*, written in collaboration with a Mexican friend, Aurora Labastida. Their aim was to present the real Mexico, as opposed to the stereotype found in many children's books. Because 70 per cent of all Mexicans live in cities, they set their story in a city and used many Mexicans as their models. "The Mexican reaction has been one of delight in recognizing themselves in the book," says Mrs. Ets, "even though some of them are in unfamiliar places and doing thing with people they never saw before."

Since the publication of *Nine Days to Christmas,* Marie Hall Ets, from her home in New York City, continues to produce a variety of appealing books, the latest being *The Elephant in the Well,* 1972. And as her work is also appearing in paperback editions, her well-deserved popularity continues to grow and widen.

LUDWIG BEMELMANS

THE SWISS HAVE a saying: "Only the best man is good enough to keep a café, a restaurant, or a hotel." Ludwig Bemelmans' Uncle Hans, a Bavarian, was of the same mind. Proud owner of a chain of inns, he made strenuous efforts to turn Ludwig into an innkeeper—and almost succeeded. Ludwig once escaped by enlisting in the United States Army during World War I. But after demobilization, he went back into the hotel business, even becoming part owner of a New York City hotel in 1925.

That he eventually became a famous author-illustrator is due to May Massee of Viking Press. On a visit to Ludwig's apartment, she noticed that the homesick young man had painted Tyrolean landscapes on his drawn shades. He had also made up for a lack of furniture by painting some elegant pieces on his walls. Miss Massee was struck by his talent and imagination. Surely, with such gifts, this young man could be a painter, or writer—or both?

During dinner, "with the help of a folded napkin, she showed him how a book should go; he could have colored pictures on the cover and here, here, and here; black and white pictures would go anywhere he liked."

Ludwig was fascinated. He had always wanted to "make pictures." The hotel business receded as he began to carve out a new and congenial career in the writing and illustrating of books for adults and children.

Ludwig Bemelmans was born on April 27, 1898, in a hotel in the Austrian (now Italian) Tyrol. His father, a Belgian painter, was what Uncle Hans called a *lump,* easy-going and "rather ne'er-do-well." His wife, the daughter of a rich brewer, divorced him after he ran away with his son's French governess.

During his childhood, Ludwig lived for years in the hotels of various countries. The life of a hotel child, with its sophistication and its transient quality, is lonely and artificial. In a world of adults, Ludwig led what seemed to him an unreal existence. "The hotel was like an all-day theatre performance," he says in *Father, Dear Father,* ". . . the upstairs was a collection of Russian grand dukes and French countesses, English lords and American millionaires. Backstairs there were French cooks, Roumanian hairdressers, Chinese manicurists, Italian bootblacks, Swiss managers, English valets."

Real life meant his other life, lived to the full on days when he escaped from the hotel to play with the children of Tyrolean peasants and workmen. Real life was the Dolomite Valley, where there was band music in the lake shore pavilion, skating in winter, and crocuses to pick in the wet, spring fields. There was a sawmill remembered so fondly that, at twenty-seven, he went back and bought it.

After his parents' divorce, Ludwig and his mother lived with her father in the old quarter of Regensburg, a little provincial town on the Danube. Ludwig was sent to public school, where they found him incorrigible. Incredibly, he was then dispatched to a private school for retarded boys.

When he was expelled, his formal schooling came to an end.

His grandfather, not at all displeased, proposed to make a brewer out of him, but his mother objected tearfully. It was then that he was sent to Uncle Hans Bemelmans' flower-covered mountain hotel, in Klobenstein, where his Aunt Marie proceeded to make much of him. After seeing some of his drawings and water colors, she suggested that he should be given art lessons, but Uncle Hans refused to consider such an idea. "Painters," he said, "were hunger candidates." He decided that Ludwig should work in the hotel, with the prospect of becoming an innkeeper.

Ludwig showed such a genius for getting into trouble that he was moved from one hotel to another—"in the space of a year, I ran through all of Uncle Hans' hotels," he says in *Life Class*. "Every manager was tried out on me; they all failed and sent me back." One day he assaulted a headwaiter who had been cruel to him, and the police were called in. Uncle Hans was given the choice of sending his nephew to reform school or to America. Ludwig chose America. When he said good-bye, his mother, more prophetic than she knew, told him, "Everything will come out all right, Ludwig."

In December, 1914, Ludwig Bemelmans, sixteen, landed in America, armed with letters of introduction to hotel men —and a brace of pistols to protect himself against Indians. "I had read of them in the books of Karl May and Fenimore Cooper, and intently hoped for their presence without number on the outskirts of New York City," he explained later.

In his first job, at the Hotel Astor, he disgraced himself by wearing one white shoe and one black, and by telling the headwaiter to go to the devil. He fared better at the Splendide, where he cultivated a taste for exotic foods and helped himself liberally to the purple Belgian grapes which he was supposed to serve daily to a distinguished guest.

New York City had its attractions, like the elevated railway, the bridges, and fishing trips with "Mr. Sigzag," a little Bohemian waiter whose true name was unpronounceable. But Ludwig was homesick for Regensburg. To comfort himself, he worked on a painting of his grandfather's brewery at night. When he took it to be framed in an art shop on Fifth Avenue, the old clerk told him he should study painting and sent him to a German artist named Thaddeus.

In the studio, impressed though he was by his teacher, the students, and the models, a paralyzing inability overcame Ludwig. Thaddeus, a fine and wise teacher, was not disturbed. He said, "Just sit and look, drink it up. . . ." Although Ludwig never drew a line during classes, he "learned to see" for the first time.

In a desperate attempt to get away from hotel work, he enlisted in the army halfway through World War One. He did not go overseas; he was an attendant in a mental hospital and a teacher of German-speaking recruits. Although the life was not much of an improvement over hotel life, he kept his sense of humor and later wrote a dryly amusing account of his experiences in *My War with the United States*.

After the Armistice, there was no chance of returning to Bavaria, as he had hoped to do. His grandfather's brewery had been lost after the war, and his mother had only the little villa in Schliersee. Ludwig became Mr. Siszag's associate in the banquet department of the Hotel Splendide. In *Life Class* he wryly recalls his activities at Jewish wedding receptions, Japanese business dinners in private suites, coming out parties, and charity cotillions.

73

During the 1920's and early 1930's he continued in hotel work—but he also drew pictures and began to receive some recognition as an artist. The turning point came at his meeting with May Massee, the start of a long and happy association with Viking Press.

His first book, *Hansi*, 1934, was a story of the Austrian Tyrol. A boy with whom all children can relate, Hansi spends Christmas with his uncle in his mountain home, joining in the celebrations of the woodchoppers, mountain climbers, and villagers.

In 1935, Ludwig married Madeline Freund, and in the following year his *Golden Basket* was a runner-up for the Newbery Medal. A lively tale of two English girls who visit the Hotel of the Golden Basket in Bruges, it is livened by some of the eccentric guests remembered from Ludwig's hotel childhood. More important, it introduces Madeline, who characteristically breaks ranks as she and her schoolmates march in "crocodile" through the cathedral.

Although these books and his *Quito Express*, 1938, are fresh and colorful, they made no great stir. But with his next book, *Madeline*, 1939, Bemelmans met success head on. With its gay, brief text and bold illustrations, *Madeline* captivated young readers. Here were pictures they understood, pictures astonishingly like those they made themselves, "first a slap, then a splash, and then a quick stroke to-finish up." The youngest of the twelve little girls in her school in Paris, Madeline is a dauntless rebel. The others envy her, even when she has appendicitis. Seeing her enthroned with flowers and candy—and the scar which she dramatically uncovers—they cry, "Boo-hoo, we want to have our appendix out, too!"

With *Madeline* a runner-up for the Caldecott Medal, Bemelmans soon became a full-fledged writer and illustrator,
traveling in Europe and the Americas and as far afield as the
Galapagos Islands. In *Father, Dear Father,* 1953, he details
his travels with his only child, Barbara (and Little Bit, her
memorable dog), pausing for tales and anecdotes, for the
story of Mr. Reallybig, and for digressions on such improbable subjects as the usefulness of volcanoes.

Everything he saw, heard, or did was grist for his mill. Besides books, he wrote articles and stories, and did illustrations, for such leading magazines as *Harper's Bazaar,
Fortune, Town and Country, Vogue, Holiday,* etc. But
these, although always perceptive and amusing, were jour-
nalism, and ephemeral. His fame rests on his picture books,
which proved a major influence on the art of juvenile illustrating.

Most popular are the Madeline books, which Bemelmans
referred to as his "old-age insurance." One of the five is
Madeline's Rescue, which won the Caldecott Medal in 1954.
In this story, Madeline says "Pooh-pooh" once too often. She
falls into the Seine, but is fished out by "a dog that kept its
head." The dog is adopted by the girls, who name her Genevieve. When Lord Cucuface, a school trustee, chases Genevieve away, the girls look for her far and wide. Genevieve returns of her own accord, and poses a problem. Whose bed
shall she sleep under? Keeping her head again, Genevieve
settles the matter by producing twelve puppies.

Madeline and the Bad Hat, 1956, and *Madeline and the
Gypsies,* 1959, are something less than Bemelman's best, al-
though young readers find no fault in them. Like all the
Madeline books, they begin engagingly:

> In an old house in Paris
> That was covered with vines
> Lived twelve little girls
> In two straight lines.

But the story veers from Madeline and her friends to the horrific doings of the "bad hat," the Spanish ambassador's son. He builds a guillotine, decapitates the chef's chickens, and goes off with a cat in a sack, pursued by the dogs of Paris. The text, though inventive, is somewhat overlong and the rhyme occasionally falters. But the illustrations are as dashing as ever.

Madeline and the Gypsies, though marred by weak verse, is popular with children. Lost when stranded on the big heel at a Paris street fair, Madeline is rescued by gypsies, who take her off to live with them. Gypsy life suits her to a T. "Never to have to brush your teeth, And never—never—to go to sleep." But after such hair-raising adventures as being sewn into a lion's skin, Madeline is glad enough to be discovered and taken home. It is even bearable to hear her teacher saying:

> "Here is a freshly laundered shirty,
> It's better to be clean than dirty."

Madeline in London, 1961, textually the least successful of Bemelmens' books, nonetheless has a most intriguing story. On a visit to London, Madeline and the girls find a horse, retired from Her Majesty's Service, which they give to their friend Pepito, the reformed bad hat. But the horse takes off at a gallop when he hears the trumpet of the Queen's Life Guards sound its *tara tara.* The chase which ensues is a miniature guide to London. When the horse is found, asleep, Madeline suggests that they take him back to Paris with them, which they do.

> They brushed his teeth and gave him bread
> And covered him up and put him to bed.

And when their long-suffering teacher comes to turn off the light, there are "twelve upstairs and below one more."

Ludwig Bemelmans died in 1962. After his late beginning, he had enjoyed unbroken success. Each of the Madeline books has been a Junior Literary Guild selection, and together the books have sold well over a quarter of a million copies.

But Bemelmans has done more than make his own impressive contribution to children's literature. He has blazed a trail for some of the most innovative of contemporary artists. His pictures have a new, cartoon-like quality, both when restricted to simple yellows and blacks and when running the gamut of riotous colors.

His pictures, too, are full of action: Miss Clavel, running "fast and faster to the scene of the disaster"; Pepito and Madeline whirling around on the ferris wheel; the gendarmes, with their hooks, rushing to fish Madeline out of the Seine. With their wild exaggeration, brilliant color, and wayward humor, they lead straight to the zany world of such popular modern illustrators as Maurice Sendak and Dr. Seuss.

H. A. REY

THE CURIOUS THING about the author-illustrator of the *Curious George* books is that, with one exception, he writes only about animals. They have such a strong fascination for him that whenever he goes to a new town he makes first for its zoo.

It was probably the first zoo Hans Augusto Rey ever knew that aroused his interest so compellingly. That zoo was the famous Hagenbeck Zoo, in Hamburg, Germany, which, at the beginning of the twentieth century, was unlike any other zoo in the world. The animals were not caged; spectators could observe them in apparently their own environment, and at liberty.

The zoo was unusual in the variety and sometimes rarity of its inmates. Started modestly in 1848 with a few seals and a polar bear brought to Hamburg by a whaler, it was inherited by Carl Hagenbeck from his father. Carl himself was a wild animal collector and dealer who, in 1875, began to exhibit animals representative of many countries in all the large cities of Europe.

As his family lived in Hamburg, the young Hans spent much of his time in the Hagenbeck Zoo, studying the animals closely and learning to imitate the sounds they made. Many years later, in America, his wife said of him, "He is proudest of his lion roar, and once he roared for 3000 children in the Atlanta Civic Auditorium, thus making the headlines in the *Atlanta Constitution* for the first and last time."

The third of four children, H. A., as he is generally called, was born in Hamburg in 1898, the son of Alexander and Martha (Windmuller) Reyersbach. The family was conservative and prosperous, their children well cared for and educated. H. A. attended what was called a Humanistic Gymnasium where he learned, successively, Greek, Latin, French, and English. A good student, he showed exceptional facility for languages but was rather bored with the rest of the curriculum.

When he was eighteen, during World War One, he served as an ordinary soldier on the Western Front. He has one reason, at least, to be grateful for his war experience; it led, long afterward, to the writing of two books on astronomy. As a soldier, he carried a small book on astronomy in his knapsack; the long, blacked-out nights gave him plenty of opportunity for stargazing. But the text was unsatisfactory; its explanations were involved and unclear. Many years later, he was still interested in the stars—and still dissatisfied with current astronomy books. So he worked out a new way to show the constellations and wrote and illustrated *The Stars: A New Way to See Them* (1952) for adult readers. Actually, his wife says, "today's children, growing up in the space age, master it (the book) better than their elders." In 1954, he wrote an astronomy book especially for children, titling it *Find the Constellations*.

The postwar years were hard for H. A. Rey, now the age for graduate study. Inflation had started in Germany, and

there was no parental money for art classes or further education. Faced with the necessity of earning a living, H. A. designed and lithographed posters for a circus, befriending
many of the animals. He managed to attend classes at the
University of Hamburg, where he studied philosophy, anat-
omy, natural sciences, and the languages which were to be a
lifelong preoccupation.

In 1923, he decided to leave Germany. During the inflation, the mark had steadily depreciated; by November, 1923,
a single copy of the newspaper cost 200,000,000,000 marks.
Barter began to be used in place of money. Food riots broke
out, and large sections of the population were in despair.
The middle classes, to which H. A. belonged, were the hard-
est hit. With little to look forward to at home, he determined to emigrate to South America, where relatives in the
import business offered him a job.

Just before he left Germany, he met his future wife, Margret Elizabeth Waldstein, like himself a resident of Hamburg. Unlike him, Margret was to have formal art education,
studying at the Bauhaus in Dessau, the Academy of Art in
Dusseldorf, and an art school in Berlin. Talented and versatile, she not only painted but did newspaper work, wrote
copy for an advertising agency, and eventually produced at
least one "singing commercial" for television.

Meantime, in Brazil, H. A. plodded along for the next
twelve years in an uncongenial position; he wrote sales letters (which, he says, he was "not allowed to adorn with illustrations") and tried to sell bathtubs up and down the Ama-
zon River.

It was Margret who rescued him and set him on the way
to his career as author-illustrator. In 1935, she turned up in

Rio de Janeiro. Disliking the Hitler regime, she had decided
to become a photographer in Brazil. Meeting H. A., she in-
duced him to leave commerce and join her in opening an advertising agency. Four months later, they were married.
Margret shared H. A.'s love for, and interest in, animals.
In Brazil they had two little marmosets as pets. When they
left for Europe in 1936 the delicate creatures did not survive
the journey. "Although my wife knitted tiny sweaters for
them, they pulled their pullovers off," H. A. recalls.

After a leisurely and belated honeymoon, spent in roam-
ing around Europe, the pair reached Paris, where they
planned to spend four weeks but actually lived for four
years. Their home was a hotel in Montmartre, a picturesque
artists' quarter with old, winding streets, canaries in the windows, and the houses and studios of such painters as Renoir
and Van Gogh.

In Paris, H. A. was commissioned to do some humorous
drawings of a giraffe for a magazine. They were spotted by
an editor of Gallimard, a French publishing firm, who asked
whether the Reys could not use the drawings as a starting
point for a children's book. They did so, producing *Cecily
and the Nine Monkeys,* their first book. One of the monkeys
was Curious George, who was to be the inspiration for a series of books that would delight millions of children.

The Reys were happy in Paris, but World War Two, with
the threat of imminent Nazi occupation, drove them from
the city. "Thirty-six hours before the Nazis entered, we fled
from Paris on bicycles," H. A. tells, "taking along only a few
victuals and some of my manuscripts." One of the manuscripts was *Curious George.*

After several days of pedaling, they sold their bicycles to

customs officials at the French-Spanish border and continued by train to Lisbon, Portugal, then a haven for refugees. From there they went to Rio de Janeiro for a brief stay, and then to New York.

As artists who had loved Montmartre, they naturally gravitated to Greenwich Village, an old and quaint section of the city, then populated largely by writers and artists. Here, in a small apartment, they started from scratch and were immediately fortunate. "We did not know a single publisher," says Margret, "but before the week was over we had found a home for *Curious George* at Houghton Mifflin Company."

Children took at once to the diverting little monkey. Curious George, on his first appearance, has hilarious adventures until he finds a nice, safe home in a zoo. The book's brightly colored, flat pictures are full of humor and action. Nancy Larrick, advising parents upon how to wean children from the comics, suggests *Curious George,* among other books, as an irresistible substitute.

In 1946, H. A. and Margret became American citizens. After twenty-three years in Greenwich Village, urban existence had lost its charm. So the Reys moved to Cambridge, Massachusetts, and also acquired a cottage in New Hampshire where they spent much of their time.

Between 1941 and 1966, H. A. wrote a series of books featuring Curious George; these included *Curious George Takes a Job,* 1947; *Curious George Rides a Bike,* 1952; *Curious George Gets a Medal,* 1957; *Curious George Learns the Alphabet* (an ABC book in which the letters are shaped like the animals and objects they stand for), 1961; and *Curious George Goes to the Hospital,* 1966.

No slickly-turned-out series books, the Curious George stories are all carefully planned and written and illustrated with scrupulous care. "People sometimes think we dash them off," says Margret. "We wish we could. We work very long on each one, frequently over a year. We write and re-write, we draw and re-draw, we fight over the plot, the beginning, the ending, the illustrations."

Prime favorites with children are *Curious George Gets a Medal* and *Curious George Rides a Bike*. The latter book is receiving special attention during the current craze for bicycling. Curious George, a show-off on his new bike, at first helps a newspaper boy to deliver his papers. But "when he came to the last house he saw a little river in the distance. George was curious: he wanted to know what the river was like, so instead of turning back to deliver the rest of the papers he just went on." His readers are not too surprised when George lands in a traveling circus as a daring rider, causes trouble for an ostrich, and redeems himself by rescuing a runaway bear.

Children identify the author so strongly with Curious George himself, Margret says, that one little boy, on meeting the Reys, was disillusioned. "I thought you were monkeys, too," he told them.

While Margret is an author in her own right (*Pretzel* and *Spotty,* among others, are her own work), the Reys also collaborate on certain books. But theirs is no cut-and-dried collaboration, with an equal division of labor. In general, Margret writes and H. A. illustrates (as in *Feed the Animals, Look for the Letters, Pretzel and the Puppies*). But sometimes Margret will write a book from an idea generated by her husband. And sometimes, when H. A. is illustrating one of Margret's books, he may make changes in the story to suit his pictures. Although his astronomy books are his own work, Margret is sometimes called upon to clarify a section or two.

The *Curious George* books have all been published in England in the *Zozo* series. These, and many of the Reys' other books, have been translated into nine languages, including Swedish, Dutch, Japanese, and Portuguese. The Reys enjoy browsing through these foreign editions. "It does not matter much that there are some we cannot read, such as Finnish and Japanese—" says Margret, "it so happens that we know the story."

ROGER DUVOISIN

O_F FRENCH SWISS ancestry, Roger Duvoisin was born on
August 28 1904, in Geneva, the ancient and beautifully situ-
ated capital of Switzerland. His is the perfect homeland in
which to bring up an artist, for Switzerland is remarkable
for its natural beauties, its spirit of freedom, and its respect
for things of the intellect. It has its poets, authors, and dram-
atists, and its artists in many fields, men like Le Corbusier,
the architect; Paul Klee, the modernist painter; Giacometti,
the great artist and sculptor. But Switzerland is unusual in
that, while some of its famous sons live and work in their native land, many others settle abroad, notably in Paris. The
adult Roger Duvoisin chose to adopt the United States as his
country.

As a boy, he was fortunate in his relatives and in the family friends, all of whom were in some way connected with
the arts. This made for a sympathetic milieu, where Roger's
talent for drawing was early recognized and encouraged. He
tells how, as a child, he loved to draw galloping horses but
could never manage to make their hoofs look real—"they always looked like oversized shoes." But he had an uncle with
a flair for drawing horses. Whenever this uncle came to visit,
Roger made him draw hundreds of horses, "prancing on elegant hoofs."

Usually to be found with his nose in a book, the young Roger had to be chased outdoors with his brothers and sisters. But even a developing passion for nature and animals did not cure his bookworm tendency. He read, in French, the classics of many countries, but he also read whatever little paper books he could buy for pennies. While not as garish as American comics, they were rather lurid. But they did him no harm; on the contrary he soon learned to judge what was worthwhile in children's literature and what was not.

There was considerable discussion in the family about what Roger should become. His father wanted him to be a chemist. His godmother thought he would do well as a painter of enamels, a field in which she herself was distinguished. Roger and his mother vetoed both ideas, but a compromise was reached. He should go in for mural painting and stage scenery designing.

He was given an exceptionally thorough education for an art career, all of it in the fine, state-owned schools and universities of Switzerland. He did his basic studies in the *collège moderne,* roughly the equivalent of high school plus two years of American college. Here the emphasis on technical teaching prepared him for specialized study at the Ecole des Arts Decoratifs, an independent branch of the larger Ecole des Arts et Metiers. For five years, he studied art and allied subjects—art history, mural painting, scenery painting, pertinent crafts, and the like.

He began his career by designing and painting scenery for the Geneva Opera Company, gaining indispensable practical experience. Besides his job in the workshop, he did illustrations and made posters. The latter were genuinely artistic; in Switzerland, poster art had reached a high peak of perfection, notably through the work of Théophile Alexandre Steinlen, the French-Swiss artist.

Roger's uncle had a friend who was manager of the largest film company in France. Good scenic designers were rare, and his uncle felt that Roger's talents would be appreciated. A change of scene was always welcome, so Roger set off for Paris with letters of introduction. After a few days, he left without going near a studio. He realized that he could not bear to be cooped up on a movie lot, far from the countryside and animals which he loved.

Another of his interests was ceramics, in which he had become fairly expert. So he was delighted when he received the offer of a position as manager of an old pottery factory, originally founded by the great French writer Voltaire. The pottery was located in the little town of Ferney-Voltaire, in beautiful farming land at the foot of the Jura Mountains, four miles southwest of Geneva.

The surroundings pleased Roger and he would have stayed indefinitely, but the old manager, jealous of the newcomer, began to harass him. He "broke pieces at night, mixed up the orders, and even threatened to cut Roger Duvoisin's throat one dark night," says Joanna Foster, in a biographical sketch.

Regretfully, Roger left to design textiles in Lyons, a commercial town on the Rhone River, famous for its many sided silk-manufacturing industry. From there he moved on to Paris, where a tempting offer changed his life. The manager of Mallinson's, an American textile company, was in Europe, scouting for talent. He liked Roger's designs, and proposed to pay his fare to the United States, provided Roger would agree to work for Mallinson's for at least four years.

Roger had recently married Louise Fatio, a native of Lausanne, Switzerland, a gay, companionable young woman who shared his interests and was later to become an author in her own right. Deciding that a few years in America would be stimulating, they agreed that Roger should accept Mallinson's offer.

Sailing to New York City, they found an apartment in Brooklyn, a sprawling borough with pleasant residential sections. Roger was pleased to find that a former college friend was already working for Mallinson's. The pair seem to have been allowed plenty of liberty. "They (Mallinson's) were very nice to us," Roger told interviewer Ruth E. Kane. "They used to say how much they would appreciate it if we could take an hour and a half instead of three hours for lunch, and that it would be a great favor if we should come to work at 9:30 instead of eleven."

This happy state of affairs came to an end three years later, when the firm went bankrupt during the Great Depression of the thirties. Roger, jobless, nevertheless decided against returning to Europe. He also determined never again to take a routine job. Instead, he would try to write and illustrate children's books, a dream he had quietly cherished for some years. He had already written two books in his spare time.

Scribner's published the first of these, *A Little Boy Drawing,* in 1932. Believing that a juvenile writer should return in imagination to the world of childhood, Roger had used an unusual technique, actually imitating the drawing style of his young son.

Nineteen-thirty-eight was a memorable year. The Duvoisins became citizens of the United States and began to design and build their future home in the hilly region of Somerset, New Jersey. "This is really countryside," wrote Ruth E. Kane, who visited them later, "barking foxes can be heard at twilight, and weasels regularly visit the Duvoisin chicken coops." She describes their home, on which Roger did much of the work himself, as "a Swiss-modernistic house, uniquely and artistically different from the typical early American farmhouses in which the area abounds."

In that same year, Duvoisin's *And There Was America* was published. A tribute to his new country, it tells of the early explorers, from Leif Erickson to the first colonists of Plymouth and Jamestown.

In the years to come, Duvoisin was to write and illustrate some thirty books for children. In addition, he has illustrated more than sixty books for others, some by his wife, some by his contemporaries, some classics, and some collections of fairy tales and legends.

In Switzerland, it is said, "art as applied to daily life has reached a singular perfection," from the painted cupboards and carved cradles of the peasant to the commercial art of window display. A true son of his native Switzerland, Duvoisin had gained experience in many fields of applied art. Through this, he developed great versatility of style, ranging from the clear-cut brilliance of the pictures in *White Snow, Bright Snow* to the sketchy line drawings of his *Petunia* books. Deliberately childlike and funny, the latter are perfectly in tune with the misdirected antics of the haughty goose.

Writing for various ages, Duvoisin adapts his illustrations to the understanding of the reader. *A for the Ark,* an animal alphabet book, holds small readers entranced. With the

Flood threatening, Noah calls the animals to safety in the ark. Large, double-page pictures, of striking simplicity, show them marching through the book, as the clouds darken on every page.

The *Petunia* books use black-and-white illustrations, varied with sudden outbursts of color. Written between 1950 and 1965, they include *Petunia, Petunia's Trip, Petunia and the Song, Petunia's Christmas, Petunia, Beware,* and *Petunia, I Love You.* Children, who relish pure nonsense, take the foolish goose to their hearts. How absurd she is, they think delightedly, putting on airs just because she has read a book! They look with happy scorn at the picture of Petunia, holding her head higher and higher until it stretches clear off the page.

But how admirable Petunia is in *Petunia's Christmas.* Who but she would carry wreaths slung around her neck? "Everyone wanted Petunia's wreaths. Some even asked whether they could buy her, too."

In *Favorite Fairy Tales Told in France,* Duvoisin uses patterned and stylized drawings, poster-like in their appeal. "Children should notice the unique patterns in floor coverings, grass and forest parks," says Charlotte S. Huck. "In his picture of Sleeping Beauty, an empty chair dominates the room, while Beauty is almost hidden from view in her alcove."

Duvoisin delights in drawing animals. Although he works best from imagination, it is only after close observation and detailed study of the creatures he wants to present. As a boy in Geneva, he was frustrated because the city zoo contained nothing but deer. "Consequently," says Ruth E. Kane, "he had to wait for the circus to come to town before he could draw his magnificent lions, elephants and tigers."

Today, in his New Jersey home, he can observe animals of many kinds at first hand, domestic and farmyard animals as well as the wild and predatory. For more exotic types, he visits the zoos in New York City's Central Park and in the Bronx.

Because he is an author as well as an illustrator, Duvoisin can fully satisfy the other authors for whom he illustrates. He knows what their stories need to make them leap into life, and he gives it to them generously. As a result, many books with Duvoisin illustrations have won honors and recommendations. *White Snow, Bright Snow,* by Alvin Tresselt, gained the Caldecott Medal for Duvoisin in 1948. The American Institute of Graphic Arts also chose it as one of the fifty best children's books of the year. In 1952, Natalie Carlson's *The Talking Cat and Other Stories of French Canada* and Herbert Coggins' *Bushy and Company,* both illustrated by Duvoisin, were Honor books in the *New York Herald Tribune*'s Children's Spring Book Festival.

Among his many awards, Duvoisin cherishes several for *The Happy Lion,* which he illustrated for his wife, Louise Fatio. Based on a true happening, the book tells of an amiable lion who escapes from a zoo in a small French town and roams peacefully through the streets. Duvoisin's sketches of a drolly sophisticiated lion accent the French flavor and humor of the tale. In West Germany, the book carried off a first prize, awarded by the government.

In 1956, Alvin Tresselt's *Hide and Seek Fog,* with pictures by Duvoisin, was a runner-up for the Caldecott Medal. In 1961, *The New York Times* selected Duvoisin's own book, *The Happy Hunter,* as the Best Illustrated Children's Book of the year.

Duvoisin's work has also been recognized by universities. In 1966 he was honored as the first winner of the Rutgers Award for distinguished contributions in the field of children's literature. And in 1971, the University of Southern Missouri presented him with a silver medal, struck especially for the occasion of its fourth Book Festival. The front of the medal shows Duvoisin in profile. On the reverse—as well she may—Petunia has pride of place!

THEODOR GEISEL (DR. SEUSS)

One of the nicest things about Theodor Geisel, better known as Dr. Seuss, is the way in which he has rescued little children from the paralyzing boredom of the primary reader. Thanks to him, they need no longer yawn over: "The ball is round. It is a round ball. Bob has the round ball . . ." but can enjoy real stories with real characters.

The first author to lend wings to books with a "controlled vocabulary"—a short list of permissible words—he had misgivings from the start. What could he do with a mere two hundred words? He mused, he experimented, he doodled— and eventually came up with *The Cat in the Hat*. Bearing little resemblance to the text of the primary reader, the book has humor, rhyme, imagination, and a neat plot. Children took to it so readily that, in its first three years, it sold over a million copies. Best of all, it encouraged other writers to use their wits to entertain as well as teach; today there are lively "beginner books" in a surprising number of categories.

Theodor Geisel was born on March 2, 1904, in Springfield, Massachusetts. His forebears were German; from them he inherited his drive and his perfectionism. His mother, Henrietta Seuss, was the daughter of a Springfield baker. His father ran the family brewery, but later in his life became superintendent of Springfield's Public Park system, which included a zoo. This fact may have prodded the grown Ted Geisel to write his best seller, *If I Ran the Zoo.*

After graduating from Central High School, young Ted entered Dartmouth College. Here he edited the college paper, *Jack-o-Lantern,* which he enlivened with dozens of his own cartoons. Dartmouth, which he remembers fondly and visists periodically, made him an Honorary Doctor of Humane Letters in 1956. "You singlehanded have stood as St. George between a generation of exhausted parents and the demon dragon of unexhausted children on a rainy day," said Dartmouth's president in conferring the honor. In the college archives, along with the manuscripts of Booth Tarkington, Sinclair Lewis, and Robert Frost, posterity may be startled to see the manuscript of *The 500 Hats of Bartholomew Cubbins*—by Dr. Seuss.

With vague thoughts of becoming a college instructor, Ted Geisel next went to England, where he more or less studied for a year in Lincoln College, Oxford. Here he met Helen Palmer, a Wellesley graduate, and they cured each other of homesickness.

Ted's proudest possession was his motorcycle. These machines were forbidden in the staid precincts of the university, but he did not let that deter him. He simply sped around with a pair of plucked ducks in his motorcycle basket and passed for a butcher's delivery boy. Helen went with him on some of his jaunts around the countryside, during one of which he proposed to her. The experience was literally upsetting as the machine went out of control and the pair landed in a ditch. Helen, imperturbable, accepted him anyway.

Finding formal study irksome, and chagrined to discover

that he knew less than the British students, Ted spent most of his time in drawing. As a sop to culture, he offered to illustrate a new edition of *Paradise Lost*. He was probably relieved when his offer was refused, leaving him free to spend a year at the University of Vienna and the Sorbonne, and in European travel.

In November, 1927, he returned to the United States and married Helen. As he had sold a couple of cartoons to *Judge*, a widely circulated humorous weekly, he felt confident that he could support a wife—and this he did, quickly making his name as a cartoonist of verve and originality. His work began to appear regularly in such periodicals as *College Humor, Vanity Fair, Liberty*, and *The Saturday Evening Post*. He did not put his name to it, however; instead, he bestowed a degree upon himself and signed his cartoons "Dr. Seuss."

As his wife became a successful author in her own right, the pair were soon able to afford an apartment on New York's Park Avenue. In a profile which he wrote for *The New Yorker*, E. I. Kahn, Jr., tells how the Geisel's telephone number differed in only one digit from that of the local fish store. In consequence, the Geisels often received telephone orders for fish. When this happened, Ted would simply sketch the order—a pound of smelts, a nice fresh haddock—on a piece of laundry cardboard and send it round to the fish store.

A versatile artist, Ted worked on a number of highly successful advertising campaigns, notably for the Standard Oil Company of New Jersey. Among others, he was responsible for the attention-getting series, "Quick, Henry, the Flit!"

The Viking Press, inadvertently, started Ted Geisel on his

career as an author-illustrator of children's books. They engaged him to illustrate *Boners* and *More Boners,* collections of schoolboy howlers. Amazed when he learned the amount which the author earned in royalties, Ted concluded that a mere illustrator was on the losing end. He determined that, from then on, he would write and illustrate his own books.

His first, an alphabet book, was rampant with the kind of outlandish animals that he had been doodling for years. "My animals look the way they do because I have never learned to draw," he said once. And on another occasion he added, "None of my animals have joints and none of them have balance. But when it comes to that, none of them are animals. They are people, sort of."

Unfortunately, the book did not sell; the publishers were not yet ready for the zany humor of Dr. Seuss. The author made no further attempt for four years. Then, when he offered *And to Think That I Saw It on Mulberry Street,* he was again rebuffed—by twenty-seven editors. The twenty-eighth was more perceptive. Marshall McClintock, then the new juvenile editor at Vanguard Press, saw the book and liked it. In this he showed excellent judgment; to date, the book has appeared in over twenty editions.

And to Think That I Saw It on Mulberry Street is a delightful testimony to the power of a child's imagination. The young hero, walking home on Mulberry Street, sees a cart and horse. By the time he reaches home, his fancy has magnified the incident out of all proportion—but in a way that all children can recognize. Not only children, but grownups, love this book. "I think it the cleverest book I have met with in several years," no less a personage than Beatrix Potter told Anne Carroll Moore. "The swing and merriment of the pictures and the natural truthful simplicity of the untruthfulness." Elementary school teachers dote on it; it lends itself perfectly to such exciting classroom activities as making simple "box movies" of the story, as well as "Dr. Seuss sculptures" in modeling wax. First-grade teachers use it to stimulate children's illustrations of events which could—with a little imagination—take place on their own streets.

With the coming of World War Two to Europe, Dr. Seuss' career as an author-illustrator was interrupted. He became a propaganda publicist for the Treasury Department and for other government agencies. But when America entered the war, he wanted to play a more active part. So he joined the Army and served for four years with Frank Capra's famous documentary film-making unit.

In the fall of 1944, he was shipped to France in connection with his film work, and arrived at General Omar Bradley's headquarters. It was suggested that he orient himself by taking a look at the countryside. He set off in a jeep, and soon found himself stranded for three days during the Battle of the Bulge. "Nobody came along and put up a sign 'This is the Battle of the Bulge,'" he told E. J. Kahn, Jr. "How was I supposed to know?" Later he became a lieutenant in the Army Signal Corps and was awarded the Legion of Merit for his educational films. "They were," he said, tongue in cheek, "calculated to elevate G.I. morals and morale."

Back home at the war's end, he divided his time between writing and illustrating children's books, and making films. As a film maker, he was soon distinguished. In 1947, he won an Academy Award for *Design for Death,* a documentary about the rise of the Japanese war lords. His animated cartoon, *Gerald McBoing-Boing,* also won an Oscar. He next wrote and directed a full-length musical, *The 5000 Fingers of Dr. T.* An extravaganza in the Hollywood manner, it concerned a Dr. Terwilliker, who forced his 500 pupils to practice their scales simultaneously on an enormous piano.

Although they were not drawn to the film colony, the Geisels fell in love with California and decided to make their home in La Jolla. They began by buying an abandoned watch tower on the top of Mount Soledad. Around it they built a pink stucco house, with a superb view of the Pacific. Here, says E. J. Kahn, they live modestly. "They have only one car, they have only one maid—part-time at that—and only one swimming pool." At first the author-illustrator wrote and drew wherever he could find a space. But today he has a well-equipped studio, with an impressive drafting board, and cork walls on which he can pin up work in progress.

The splendidly innovative *The Cat in the Hat,* published in 1958, came about in answer to John Hersey's plea for a readable book for the very young. Its success prompted Dr. Seuss and his wife to launch a series of Beginner Books for Random House, calling upon other authors for contributions in the same happy vein. The venture flourished from the start. Later, Random House took it over entirely, but Dr. Seuss remained the largest contributor and a substantial shareholder.

The Cat in the Hat was followed by *One Fish, Two Fish, Three Fish,* a counting book for the pre-kindergarten child, and *Green Eggs and Ham.* The latter, a huge favorite, opens challengingly:

THEODOR GEISEL (DR. SEUSS)

> Do you like
> Green eggs and ham?
> I do not like them
> Sam-I-am
> I do not like
> Green eggs and ham . . .
> I do not like them
> here or there
> I do not like them
> anywhere . . .

Another innovation was Dr. Seuss' novelty book, *My Book about Me*, 1971. In this one, the children virtually write their autobiographies, recording their vital statistics and answering questions about themselves, their homes, their families and pets. At its launching party, the invited guests were enchanted by their first venture in completing an autobiography. Peeks over shoulders, as the children scribbled and drew, revealed such truths as the following: Pamela Talese has six freckles; the Friths live in a house where there are four mirrors, ten electric lights, three cold water faucets and two hot; the Osborne brothers never talk in their sleep.

Dr. Seuss' books gained even wider popularity after three *favorites—Horton Hears a Who, How the Grinch Stole Christmas,* and *The Cat in the Hat*—were made into animated cartoons and shown on television.

Although his readers may not suspect it, all of the Seuss stories are moral tales. In *The Sneetches,* for instances, he takes his stand against snobbery. The Star-Belly Sneetches, with stars on their bellies, regrettably look down upon the Plain-Belly Sneetches. In *How the Grinch Stole Christmas,*

Dr. Seuss proves that Christmas means "a little more than just gifts and gift-giving." *Horton Hears a Who* demonstrates in conclusive fashion the author's belief that "A person is a person no matter how small."

With over thirty books to his credit, Dr. Seuss, for a change, paints an occasional mural, models his strange animals in plaster, or takes a trip. He has traveled in Europe, South Africa, and in the Near East. At home he putters in his rock garden—rock collecting is his only hobby—and autographs his books for visitors to the La Jolla bookstore.

A shy man, he is daunted by the numbers of people who try to invade his tower and grounds. Even children, although he loves and understands them, are kept at bay. He has none of his own. "You have 'em," he tells parents, "I'll amuse 'em." And this, as everyone knows, he does with ease.

LEO LIONNI

ALTHOUGH THE illustrated book has a very long history, the picture book is a recent, and quite different, form of children's literature. The former uses illustrations as an attractive accessory; it pictures the characters, happenings, and background of the story. But the illustrations are not an absolute necessity; take away the pictures and the story can stand alone, complete in its own right.

In a picture book, however, text and illustrations may be of equal importance, as in the books of Beatrix Potter. Or the pictures may dominate the text, as in Richard Scarry's work. And today, with the extraordinary development in contemporary methods of reproduction, the pictures may be so plentiful that they carry the story and little text is necessary; we even see an occasional picture book with no words at all.

For the too-young-to-read and the very young reader, the happy medium seems to be the picture book with clear, uncluttered pictures and a minimum of text. Books of this kind are the special province of Leo Lionni; in almost all his books, the pictures are arresting and immediately understandable, and the text is brief.

In *Inch by Inch,* 1960, there are often double-page pictures accompanied by as little as four words. The tiny text tells an enchanting story of an inchworm who, challenged by a robin, measures the tails of a number of birds. He then meets a nightingale—and his Waterloo. For the nightingale asks to have his *song* measured. The inchworm obliges, crawling inch by inch up a blade of grass near the robin until the song soars to such heights that he inches clear out of sight.

One of the most sophisticated of today's picture book author-illustrators, Leo Lionni was born in 1910 in Amsterdam, Holland, a city whose sixty-five canals and old red-brick houses make it eminently paintable. He was educated in a number of countries—Holland, Belgium, Switzerland, Italy—and their variety of lifestyles turned him into a cosmopolitan personality, witty and charming.

Leo had no formal art training. On the contrary, he took his Ph.D. at the University of Genoa in a subject which most artists find uncongenial—economics.

But though he is a self-made artist, he must have found much in his surroundings to help and inspire him. Amsterdam itself is a famous art center with forty museums, some vast, like the Rijksmuseum and the Stedelijk-museum, and some small but distinguished, like Rembrandt's House. Genoa, too, has fine art galleries, housed in buildings of architectural beauty.

Like his contemporary, Roger Duvoisin, Lionni felt that opportunity awaited him in the United States. So, in 1939, he came to Philadelphia to be art editor in the advertising agency of N. W. Ayer. Later, he worked for *Fortune Magazine,* the Olivetti Corporation, and the Parsons School of Design. He also did illustrations for *Ladies' Home Journal, Charm, Holiday,* and other national magazines, and served as co-editor of *Print Magazine.*

He could not have chosen a better field than commercial art. Like Dr. Seuss, the Petershams, William Steig, and many author-illustrators, this experience gave him sound and comprehensive training for his later career in children's literature. During World War Two there were many and striking innovations in printing, and commercial artists benefited greatly from them. They familiarized themselves with the new machinery and were quick to grasp its potentialities. Later, when they turned to careers which involved illustration, they were already technically proficient, ready to adopt such exciting new methods as, for example, the use of acrylics and/or collage in mixed media. (Mixed media means that the artist combines whatever suits his picture—for example, he might use charcoal, water color, and ink.)

In 1959, at a time when young readers faced a deluge of fact and information books, Lionni came out with his first offering, a folk tale. Not, however, of the usual type. *Little Blue and Little Yellow* is a modern folk tale. The pictures are completely abstract, leading some grown-ups to wonder whether children really like such illustrations. The answer is that they *do.* Even very young children, perhaps because of the stark simplicity and splashy colors of their own pictures, recognize the abstract shapes and find Lionni's colors fascinating.

In all his books, Lionni deals with animals, or with objects in nature—pebbles, mushrooms, flowers, etc. But they are never realistic; they have the reactions and characteristics of human beings. "Of course my books, like all fables, are about people," he says. "Worms don't measure, torn paper doesn't go to school, little fish don't organize, birds don't engage in philanthropy. . . . My characters are humans in disguise and their little problems and situations are human problems, human situations."

Even when he presents inanimate objects realistically, he gives them a new twist. In the highly original *On My Beach There Are Many Pebbles,* 1961, some of the pebbles have faces, others form themselves into a clock, and still others retain their basic shapes but, with a touch of the pencil, have been transformed into owls, hens, peanuts, a seal, etc.

Lionni does not write merely to entertain. His books, in general, are fables or allegories; they teach a lesson or point a moral, but with subtlety and charm. In *Swimmy,* 1963, and *Tico,* 1964, the heroes win out because of their virtues or good qualities, Swimmy because of his resourcefulness, and Tico because of his goodness. The author believes that, in writing for children, it is easier to teach through animal characters than through child characters; when presenting animals, there is no need for an elaborate and accurate background, or for the descriptive detail that is necessary when picturing a specific boy or girl.

Like Beatrix Potter, Edna Miller, and other author-illustrators, Lionni finds mice an irresistible subject. Indeed, as he once told librarian Rose Agree, who interviewed him for the *Wilson Library Bulletin,* he plans a whole series of mouse books. The underlying theme would be "the discovery of who you are, your strength as well as weakness, and how to make the best of what it is you believe you are most capable of becoming."

A grandiose conception, but not impossible for Lionni to carry out. Already his mice characters have served him well. *Frederick,* with its mouse hero, was a runner-up for the Caldecott Medal in 1968. *Alexander and the Wind-up Mouse* made Lionni a four-time contender for the medal in 1970 (he had already been a runner-up with *Inch by Inch* and *Swimmy*).

Lionni does not believe in having a particular, personal style. He suits his style to the theme and atmosphere of whatever book he is writing, and uses mixed media with extraordinary success. Examine a Lionni illustration at random and you will find more than one medium on the page— perhaps charcoal or pencil, with water color and collage.

Leo Lionni is currently living in Lavagna, Italy, where he has books in various stages of progress, and where he is also experimenting with film-making. His books, however, come first; they satisfy him as no other work has done.

In both his commercial and literary careers, he has won a large number of honors. In 1955 he was named "Art Director of the Year" by the National Society of Art Directors. In 1956, the Architectural League awarded him their Gold Medal for Architecture. His children's books have gained recognition both nationally and internationally, winning not only literary awards but awards for excellence in design. They have also appeared on annual lists of the best illustrated books, such as that compiled by *The New York Times*.

And, as if this were not enough, this unusually brilliant author-illustrator has had one-man exhibitions of his paintings in many museums and galleries both in Europe and the United States.

ROBERT McCLOSKEY

To GET THEIR full flavor, the books of Robert McCloskey should be read at just the right age. *Make Way for Ducklings,* for instance, is the picture book par excellence for reading in the first and second grades. No other age group would be so concerned about Mrs. Mallard and her ducklings as they brave the Boston traffic. And how these small children would enjoy hearing that the author kept six ducklings in the bathtub of his New York City apartment while he made sketches! How absurd they would find the idea—and how they would love it!

Homer Price, too, is best appreciated by boys and girls at a special stage, the stage that relishes tall tales and wild exaggeration. The innocently outrageous Homer does things which they would give a lot to do themselves. He captures four robbers single-handed and marches them up Main Street in their pyjamas. He tames a skunk and calls her Aroma. He fills Uncle Ulysses' lunchroom with "a calamity of doughnuts" because he cannot stop the machine.

Time of Wonder, which captures the changing moods of the Maine coast, makes its appeal to "young and old alike who have ever intensely loved a particular place on earth. Words and pictures complement each other so perfectly," says Charlotte S. Huck, "that the reader is filled with quiet wonder and nostalgia."

Born in Hamilton, Ohio, on September 15, 1914, Robert McCloskey is easily discernible in his work. The eight books which he wrote and illustrated mirror his life closely. Even the most exaggerated have the ring of truth, and are rich in his humor and love of life. As a schoolboy, he had a variety of ambitions. He took to music like a duck to water. He played the piano, the oboe, and the drums, and was a virtuoso on the harmonica. He toyed with the notion of becoming a musician but changed his mind when he found he could invent things. He worked wonders with bits of wire, the innards of old clocks, and bits from Erecto sets. One of his gadgets, a machine for whipping cream, worked so furiously that most of the cream landed on the kitchen walls.

The young Robert McCloskey had an affinity with youth, especially boys, and his experiences in coaching and counseling gave him an amused but sympathetic insight into the ways boys think and act. As a teen-ager, he taught hobbies at the YMCA after school hours, teaching boys how to play the harmonica, do soap carving, and make model airplanes.

During this time he was also drawing for his school paper and yearbook, and his ambition changed again. He would be an artist. Winning a scholarship to the Vesper George School of Art in Boston, he studied there for three winters; during the summers he was a counselor in a boys' camp.

Two years after entering art school, he got his first commission, executing the bas-reliefs (shallow carvings) on the municipal building of his home town.

In 1935, he went to New York City, where he showed some of his work to May Massee at Viking Press. His grandiose conceptions did not impress her; his lack of technique did. "I don't remember just what words she used to tell me to get wise to myself and shelve the dragons, Pegasus, limpid pool business, and learn what to 'art' with," McCloskey said later. But he took her advice, studying for the next two years at the National Academy of Design. During the summer he studied and painted in Provincetown, an artists' haunt on the tip of Cape Cod, famed for the beauty of its sand dunes and marine views. Here he sold a few water colors but had to depend upon uncongenial commercial art to pay his expenses.

With May Massee's counsel still in mind, he returned to Ohio, where he concentrated on drawing and painting the small-town life around him. This resulted in his first book, *Lentil,* 1940, a humorous story illustrated with large caricatures. Young Lentil lives in Alto, Ohio, a town much like Hamilton. He longs to sing but cannot even whistle— because he can't pucker his lips. He buys a harmonica and, like McCloskey in his youth, becomes so expert that he saves the day with his musical welcome when Colonel Carter, the town's benefactor, comes to visit. The book ends with the author's laconic comment, "You never can tell what will happen when you learn to play a harmonica."

McCloskey took the book to May Massee, and Viking Press accepted it for publication. His career off to a good start, he then married Margaret Durand, daughter of author Ruth Sawyer. In the following year, he scored his first big success with *Make Way for Ducklings,* which won the Caldecott Award for the most distinguished picture book of 1941.

He had prepared for this book with praiseworthy thoroughness and considerable relish. During his years at art school, he had noticed the ducklings in Boston's Public Gardens, but had not thought to draw them. Four years later, on a return visit to Boston, he noticed the ducklings' predicament with traffic, and conceived the idea of a picture book about their plight. For some days he visited the ducks, studying their movements closely. Back in New York City, he went to the American Museum of Natural History, where he was allowed to examine and sketch two stuffed mallards and their nests. As noted earlier, he even bought some live ducklings to use as models in his apartment—but the creatures were too lively. "I had to slow down those ducks somehow so I could make the sketches," he recalls. "The only thing that worked was red wine. They loved it and went into slow motion right away."

In 1943, *Homer Price* was published. In the six tall tales of Homer's adventures, there is much to remind the reader of McCloskey's own boyhood. His early interest in wild inventions, for instance, stood him in good stead when he came to write about Homer's experiences with Uncle Ulysses' automatic doughnut-maker and Mike Murphy's musical mousetrap.

Later in 1943, McCloskey joined the army. A sergeant, he was sent to Fort McClellan, in Alabama, where he stayed for three years. Of his work there, which included the making of visual aids, he says mock-seriously, "My greatest contribution to the war effort was inventing a machine to enable short lieutenants to flip over large training charts in a high breeze."

In 1948, with his wife and two daughters, Sally and Jane, McCloskey spent a year in Italy. Attracted by the idea of a new medium, he studied mosaic-making. In this intricate art, minute pieces of stone, glass, marble, etc., of different colors and shapes, are joined together to produce a colorful and pleasing effect.

Except for a visit to Mexico, the next twenty years were largely spent in Maine, where the McCloskeys had their own island home near Cape Rosier. Family life in Maine gave him the material for several of his most important books. *Blueberries for Sal,* 1948, illustrated in blue and white, was a runner-up for the Caldecott Award. It tells how small Sal, a tousled imp, goes with her mother to pick blueberries for canning. Sal wanders off, eating as she goes, and manages to lose her mother. She comes upon a mother crow, a mother bear, and a mother partridge, each with their young. Eventually, "Little Bear and Little Sal's mother and Little Sal and Little Bear's mother were all mixed up with each other among the blueberries on Blueberry Hill." They reach home safely—Little Sal had been unconscious of danger—to start canning in their kitchen which, with the exception of the old iron stove, is the McCloskey's own kitchen.

One Morning in Maine, 1952, starts with Sal growing up and losing her first tooth, a tragi-comic experience with which young readers quickly identify. The whole family appears in the story, and the understanding of the parents is warmly sensed. The pets, too, ramble in and out of the pages; Mozzarella, the black cat, and Penny, the setter. The village where they shop is modeled after the village store to which the McCloskeys go by rowboat to fetch supplies.

Time of Wonder, 1958, won a second Caldecott Award for its author-illustrator. The rhythmic text and softly colored pictures wander over the landscape of Mr. McCloskey's island, impressing young readers with the beauty of land, sky, and water, and acquainting them with its people, animals, and plants. The weather plays an important part, changing mood and scene as the fog lifts, the hurricane blows, or winter winds grip the island. In this book, for the first time, McCloskey uses deep water colors; he aims, not at realism, but at conveying an atmosphere of quiet and mystery. The family's own delight and wonder are recaptured as the author-illustrator invites the reader:

> Take a farewell look
> at the waves and sky.
> Take a farewell sniff
> of the salty sea.
> A little bit sad
> about the place you are leaving,
> a little bit glad
> about the place you are going.
> It is a time of quiet wonder—
> for wondering, for instance:
> Where do the hummingbirds go
> in a hurricane?

With Homer Price well on his way to becoming the legendary hero of all-American boys, McCloskey wrote a second book of his adventures in *Centerburg Tales,* 1951. Here again is small-town life, real but magnified and highly colored, as lived by Homer and his friends. Together, *Homer Price* and *Centerburg Tales* form what is probably the classic among modern humorous stories.

In 1963, McCloskey brought out the last of his Maine tales, *Burt Dow: Deep-Water Man.* The bold, richly colored pictures are full of movement and wild humor. A whale gives Burt a Jonah-like refuge in his tummy in gratitude for a peppermint-striped bandaid which Burt kindly applied to his wounded tail. In this fine farrago of nonsense, Burt, in his dory, *Tidley Idley,* navigates "the length of the gullet and into the whale's tummy without so much as touching a tonsil." The tallest of sea stories, this one is happily preposterous, the more so because the author-illustrator tells us that Burt is a real person who once sailed vessels around the globe.

In 1964, McCloskey was recognized in his home state with an honorary degree of Doctor of Literature from Miami University, Oxford, Ohio, a degree well deserved for his carefully conceived and meticulously illustrated books.

As was to happen in the case of Maurice Sendak's *Where the Wild Things Are,* people of limited imagination and understanding were to look askance at Homer Price. Phyllis Fenner, in *The Proof of the Pudding,* tells of a mother at a book fair who would not let her son buy the copy of *Homer Price* that he was begging for. "He was the kind of boy who would have benefited by it," says Miss Fenner. "He needed the humor of Homer."

Children, for the most part, relish funny stories. They love pure nonsense. They like to laugh. And today, in a land "fast acquiring an environment of machines, by machines, for machines," that laughter has become a very special need. Robert McCloskey, with his special brand of humorous realism, is filling that need.

BRINTON TURKLE

THE FACT THAT Brinton Turkle is a Quaker has much to do with the gently implied lessons in his books—lessons which are unusually pertinent today. From their beginning, Quakers have followed the words of Christ to the letter, opposing war and advocating relief for the poor, but stressing self-help.

As a writer, Brinton Turkle wants to entertain, and this he does with originality, humor, and charm. As a Quaker, he means to do more; he wants to leave his young readers with an appreciation of such virtues as integrity, tolerance, kindness, and reverence for God's creatures and His creation. He will feel compensated, he once said, if "having read *The Fiddler of High Lonesome,* one child feels it impossible to pull the trigger."

The son of Edgar Harold Turkle, a funeral director, and Ada Turkle, Brinton was born on August 15, 1915, in the small manufacturing city of Alliance, Ohio. As a boy, he went to public school, where he could not work up much interest in anything but drawing. He was constantly punished for inattention, but this did not stop him from drawing happily during class.

Although Alliance has a college, Mount Union, which all the other members of his family attended, Brinton decided to do otherwise. He rightly sensed that he needed art training. Fortunately his parents were understanding; they helped him through his first years at the Carnegie Institute of Technology (today the Carnegie-Mellon University). After this he continued his art training at the School of the Boston Museum of Art until 1940.

Brinton Turkle is one of those rare author-illustrators who knew from the start exactly what he wanted to do. He did not dabble in this or that. "I seem to have aimed my career with a remarkable singleness of purpose," he said in an article in *Publishers Weekly.* "I never wanted to do easel painting or make prints or do anything but illustrate books."

After four years in Boston, he showed some of his drawings, and a short story, to several New York editors. They were impressed—but not enough. When they advised him to return after he had gained some experience, he headed for Chicago to work in the advertising field.

Commercial art eventually enabled him to earn a good living—until his Quaker conscience caught up with him. Sometimes he knew, or sensed, that the product which his employer was advertising was shoddy or of poor quality; the thought that his artwork was helping to deceive the buying public began to disturb him.

At this point he decided to go to New Mexico, make a living as a book illustrator, and ponder the possibility of settling down and becoming a family man.

Everything worked out according to plan. He married in 1948 and in time had three children, Matilda, Haynes, and Jonathan, now grown. His illustrating was successful from the start, and the variety of the books he illustrated gave him excellent practice for his later career.

His first book, *Obadiah the Bold*, 1965, was the direct result of a visit to Nantucket, an island south of Cape Cod which still retains the old atmosphere of its days of Quaker dominance. This atmosphere surprised and impressed Brinton Turkle, and he awoke one morning with a Quaker story in his head. He decided to write it down. Its hero would be the bashful, redheaded little Quaker boy whom he had recently drawn as a Valentine for a small friend.

At the suggestion of a fellow author, Ezra Jack Keats, he submitted the finished story to Viking Press. Here, to his surprise and gratification, it was accepted with flattering promptness. When it appeared, critics praised the book warmly and one of them, Lavinia Russ of *Publishers Weekly*, went so far as to call it "the perfect picture book."

He dedicated the book to his youngest son, Jonathan, telling him how his name would be in the front of the book, and how the book would be included in libraries all over the United States.

To his chagrin, Jonathan dismissed the honor in cavalier fashion. "Okay, Daddy," he said. "I don't mind."

For his second book, *The Magic of Millicent Musgrave*, 1967, Brinton Turkle looked back to the days of his childhood, remembering his disgust when a small girl friend was promised a rabbit by a party magician—and received a doll. The Millicent of his book fares better; she and her father chase the cheating magician to Europe, having wonderful adventures en route. And, although she doesn't get the rabbit, she gets something better—she realizes that she loves her doll, and that love demands loyalty.

The Magic of Millicent Musgrave was a success. Reviewers, as well as children, responded to its gaiety and warmth. Its illustrations are as appealing as the text; drawings in soft pink and gray, they evoke the quaint charm of Edwardian days, when little girls like Millicent wore party frocks with big sashes, and ladies wore hats with flowers and veiling.

In the course of time, Brinton Turkle gravitated from New Mexico to New York City, where he soon found himself in demand as a speaker at book fairs, and in schools and libraries. While not much relishing the "chalk talks" he was asked to give, he liked and enjoyed his young audiences and went to considerable trouble to keep them entertained.

The results were sometimes amusing. Once, in Cleveland, he pretended that one of his book characters was alive and with him. Taking him by his imaginary hand, Brinton asked him to sit down while he drew his portrait. Then Brinton went to the blackboard and sketched the character.

The children had mixed reactions to the imaginary figure. A few roundly declared that there was nobody there. Others were uncertain. Some really believed that they saw the figure. But one boy, to Brinton's amusement, answered solemnly, "That's the first time I ever saw an artist draw a ghost!"

In 1969, a sequel to *Obadiah the Bold* was published and was a runner-up for the Caldecott Award. Titled *Thy Friend, Obadiah,* it is a telling story of how a young boy learns the meaning of true friendship. Impatient with a seagull which follows him around and makes him look ridiculous, he longs to be rid of it. But when the "silly old bird" needs his help, Obadiah hurries to give it. Finally, he concludes, "That seagull is my friend. . . . Since I helped him, I'm *his* friend."

The author's next book, *The Sky Dog,* 1969, was equally successful. He followed it with *Mooncoin Castle,* 1970, a book for older children. The idea for the story came to him when, during a visit to Ireland (a country he loved at sight), he saw an old castle, in need of restoration. In *Mooncoin Castle,* he writes of just such a building. However, this castle is peopled with birds and a ghost who have no intention of allowing their home to be destroyed.

Today, Brinton Turkle lives and works in New York City, where he is currently writing and illustrating a contemporary picture book. He is also considering a book on racism. In his spare time, he enjoys the theater, both Broadway and off-Broadway. Another hobby is music; he likes classical recordings and can play the piano himself—well, but "by ear."

Travel has been a long-term hobby. He has visited most of the United States, with the exception of the Deep South, and has been to England, France, and Germany. It is Ireland, though, to which he is chiefly drawn. "I've been in Ireland three times," he says, "and I hope to live there some day soon."

But no matter where he goes or what he does, Brinton Turkle continues to live up to his Quaker convictions. Recently, he was as bold as his own Obadiah; he refused to pay his income taxes, believing that they were helping America to fight the Vietnam war. He was even prepared to face a prison sentence, which would probably have ruined his career as an author-illustrator for children.

Fortunately, prison did not eventuate, and the war came to an end. So Brinton Turkle is free to plan books, write, and illustrate, and dream of a happy future—in the Emerald Isle.

MARCIA BROWN

Wɪᴛʜ ᴍᴏsᴛ illustrators, it takes only a short time to learn to recognize their particular styles. No one, for instance, could mistake a Beatrix Potter landscape for one of Wanda Gág's, or Kate Greenaway's Lucy Locket for Ludwig Bemelmans' Madeline. But we are brought up short if we try to pinpoint the style of Marcia Brown. Like Marie Hall Ets, she has not one, but several, and each is peculiarly adapted to the tale she tells.

For the make-believe world of *Cinderella,* she uses the lightest of brush strokes, the most evanescent of colors. Only the features of the characters—especially the beaky noses and receding chins of the ugly sisters—are sharply etched. In *Dick Whittington and His Cat* the style is completely different; the pictures are linoleum cuts in brown and black— bold, vigorous, and as full of movement as the story itself. Each of her books has its special medium—line drawing, woodcut, gouache (a way of painting in opaque colors ground in water and thickened with gum and honey), and others.

This versatile author-illustrator was born on July 13, 1918, in Rochester, New York. Her father was a minister, and the Browns, like ministers' families in story books, moved often, although always within the state.

One of their earliest homes was the parsonage in Coopers-town, a lovely little village at the foot of Otsego Lake in New York State. Here the Brown girls could roam safely, for the village was pleasantly remote, served by a single bus line and a railroad that carried nothing but freight. The village lay in the midst of the romantic scenes of James Fenimore Cooper's *Leatherstocking Tales—The Pioneer, The Last of the Mohicans,* etc. The girls liked to visit his grave in the Episcopalian cemetery and play among the tombstones.

Their parents knew the value of natural pleasures and encouraged their daughters to explore the woodlands and lake shore with a seeing eye. Marcia took delight in the visual. When they lived for a time near the Hudson, she liked to watch the river traffic, "the sidewheeler day boats that threw huge swells, night boats like silver fish, tugs and heavy barges . . . tankers, freighters from all over the world."

When the weather kept them indoors, the girls busied themselves "making things" like toys, sail boats, and paper dolls. Marcia, early interested in puppetry, constructed ingeniously jointed puppets in her father's workshop.

All the family liked to read, and the public library was "a second home," heady with possibilities. Marcia remembers that, after each of the family moves, she would go with her sisters to sign for her library card before her mother "had even unpacked the china." Her favorite stories were the tales of Grimm, Perrault, and Hans Andersen, but she was a bookworm and read anything that came her way.

The sisters enjoyed drawing and painting, and started young. For the small Marcia, her father painted one wall of the kitchen black, a fine area to splash colors on. As a special treat, the girls were given large drawing pads at Christmas, but paper of all kinds was put to use, from the blank spaces in magazines to the margins of school texts.

When Marcia was twelve the local librarian, impressed by her absorption in illustrated books, allowed her to examine the art books and journals in the stacks. She became familiar with the grotesque and fantastic illustrations of the French painter, Gustave Doré; with the fairy-tale pictures and cartoons of the British illustrator, Edmund Dulac; and with Arthur Rackham's water-color pictures for *Peter Pan, Rip Van Winkle, The Water Babies,* and other classics.

After her graduation from Kingston High School, Marcia trained in the New York State College for Teachers, in Albany. Every spring she "almost succumbed to the impulse to run away and go to art school," but she stayed the course, gaining a degree in English and Dramatics in 1940. During her college years she had at least the opportunity to learn and practice scene painting, and her designing and painting of stage sets won her two summer scholarships to the Woodstock School of Painting.

In spite of a nagging wish to paint, she put her teacher-training to use during three years in the Cornwall, New York, high school. Then, in 1943, she headed for New York City. She studied painting in the New School for Social Research, took classes at the Art Students League, and found a part-time job in the New York Public Library. Here, as an assistant librarian, she could examine the cream of contemporary picture books and, as a storyteller, learn much about the little people for whom she was soon to write and draw.

New York City gave her the stimulus and setting for her first book, *The Little Carousel,* 1946. She was living on Sullivan Street, in an Italian district of Greenwich Village, where she became familiar with the volatile Italian temperament and the colorful street life. On special days there would be religious festivals, with shrines in the windows and gaudy statues carried shoulder-high through the streets. Children, in perpetual motion, swarmed on roofs and fire escapes and played on the stoops and sidewalks.

To these city children, the arrival of the horse-drawn merry-go-round was an event. It proved an event to Marcia, too. "From my apartment window, I saw the little carousel arrive," she told an interviewer, "and the episode that makes the plot of the story happened before my delighted eyes." World War Two had not long ended, and the Italian neighborhood blazed with streamers in the national colors, black, red, and green. Marcia used these colors to effect in *The Little Carousel.*

During her storytelling period in the New York Public Library, she built up a stock of folk tales, fairy tales, and legends to please her young audiences. The children were of all nationalities—West Indian, Chinese, Italian, Finnish, Czechoslovakian—and her repertoire included something from each child's literary heritage. *Stone Soup,* 1947, is her version of an old French tale about three hungry soldiers, who outwit some villagers by extending the meat-and-vegetable soup with stones. Because of the restrictions which persisted for some time after the end of the war, the book was published in limited color, but its droll humor appealed to children everywhere.

Following her years in the New York Public Library, Marcia traveled widely; her trips to Mexico, Hawaii, the West Indies, and later, Europe, gave her settings and materials for her books. *Henry-Fisherman,* 1949, reflected her impressions of the island of St. Thomas, where she spent two summers. For this story, she used tropical colors—brown, chartreuse and gold, flashed with coral and turquoise. "I look at the pictures now, and wonder why, why *Henry-Fisherman* had not quite the general appeal of the other books," said her editor, Alice Dalgliesh, in a biographical sketch. "Children of the Virgin Islands in the West Indies and Negro children of this country love that appealing little brown boy who wanted so much to be a fisherman."

Dick Whittington and His Cat, 1950, is a retelling of a story that originated in an English chap book, one of those small pamphlets of tales and ballads that were once hawked about by chapmen or peddlers. Marcia's version swings along at a great pace. "Look sharp there, clean the spit, empty the dripping pan, sweep the floor," the cook cries to Dick. "And down came the ladle on the boy's shoulders. For the cook was always roasting and baking, and when the spit was still, she basted his head with a broom or anything else she could lay her hands on."

Other books followed: *Skipper John's Cook,* 1953, a Cape Cod story; *Puss in Boots,* 1953, a happy example of the contemporary practice of basing a book upon a single fairy tale; and the M. R. James retelling of *The Steadfast Tin Soldier,* 1953, for which Marcia supplied the illustrations. All three books were runners-up for the Caldecott Medal.

In 1953, Marcia was invited to give a summer course in puppetry in the University College of the West Indies. With puppets a favorite preoccupation since childhood, she accepted, gave the course in Jamaica, and then took puppet shows to small villages where they were completely novel to the children. Of the three types of puppet—marionette, operated by strings or wire from above; rod puppets, operated by rods from below; and glove puppets, operated by hand— she preferred glove puppets as being the most flexible and the easiest to handle. Some of her puppet shows were based on her own books, and her early training in dramatics stood her in good stead.

In 1954, Marcia Brown produced her treasurable *Cinderella,* which carried off the Caldecott Medal in 1955. Actually, she is not much in favor of awards, literary or otherwise. "There's too much emphasis on awards in our society," she said once. "It has no effect on our work." But naturally she enjoyed the recognition which came to her; when she was awarded the Medallion at the 1972 Festival of the University of Southern Mississippi, she received it with gratitude and pleasure.

As illustrator or author-illustrator of over twenty successful books for children, she has received numerous honors for her books and artwork. Besides receiving two Caldecott Medals, the second for *Once a Mouse,* in 1962, she has had many of her books chosen by the American Library Association for the annual list of notable children's books. Her prints have been exhibited at the Brooklyn Museum, the Carnegie Institute, and several galleries, and her work is well represented in the permanent collection of the Library of Congress.

RICHARD SCARRY

IN SPITE OF their popularity with small readers, the books of Richard Scarry are not always liked by parents or recognized by reviewers. Some form of intellectual snobbery is responsible. Many of the Scarry books are what is known as "mass market" or "merchandise" books, whose appeal is visual rather than literary. They are books of instant appeal to the young, profusely illustrated and with irresistibly bright covers.

The subjects of mass market books are never unusual or intimidating. They reflect the everyday experiences of the average child. Parents who buy them know that they are running no risk. Children will understand them and feel at home with them; what is more they are comparatively inexpensive at a time when books are highly priced.

Nowadays the boundary between the mass market book and the prestige book is not clearly defined. Increasingly, mass market books are improving in quality, widening their range of interests, and enlisting such fine and innovative writers as Dr. Seuss and Maurice Sendak. The Scarry books might be described as mass market books par excellence; they have the necessary bright covers and plentiful pictures, and they deal with such familiar subjects as supermarkets, schools, cars, trains, buses, and boats. Typical is *The Super-*

market Mystery, 1969. Except for the fact that its customers are animals, the supermarket is comfortably recognizable, with its shopping carts, checkout counters, and displays of canned goods and catsup. But there are delightful touches of imagination. One of the customers wears a hat composed of a pineapple, bananas, peaches, and pears. Another, a mouse, is pushing an infinitesimal shopping cart with a baby mouse riding proudly. Such flights of fancy fill Scarry books with surprises.

Richard Scarry was born on June 9, 1919, in Boston, Massachusetts. The son of John James and Barbara McClure Scarry, he was sent to Boston schools, where it was discovered that he had a bent for drawing. This led to a rounded art education; he attended the Archipenko Art School in New York, the Boston Museum Art School, and the Water Color School in Maine.

At twenty-two, he joined the army, where he served in a number of capacities; he was art director, editor, writer, and illustrator in the Morale Services Section, working at the Allied Forces Headquarters in the North African and Mediterranean theaters. He left the army with the rank of captain and, in 1949, married Patricia Murphy, a writer of juvenile books.

He soon found his niche in the literary marketplace. For more than twelve years, he wrote a variety of books for Golden Press, publishers of between eighty and a hundred mass market titles a year. The books were filled with amusing and highly individual little animals which, however, acted and reacted like people. "I like to draw animals," Scarry commented in *Publishers Weekly,* "and I think children can identify more closely with pictures of animals than they can with pictures of another child. . . . With imagination—and children all have marvelous imaginations —they can easily identify with an anteater who is a painter or a goat who is an Indian or a honey-bear schoolteacher."

Then, in 1963, he produced *The Best Word Book Ever,* writing in a new form, peculiarly his own. "Occasionally," says Selma G. Lanes in *Down the Rabbit Hole,* "genius will out, and a product devised hardheadedly for the mass market proves so lastingly popular that the author-illustrator becomes more important than the product he helped to produce." This was what happened in the case of *The Best Word Book Ever.* It became a best seller, and is still selling. Filled with active, comical little animals (sometimes with as many as twelve pictures to a page), it shows them engaged in the everyday activities with which all small children are familiar—walking, digging, building, eating, watching television, etc.

Richard Scarry's talent became widely recognized and *The Best Word Book Ever* proved a turning point in his career. Although he continues to write for Golden Press, his books are also published by such prestigious firms as Random House, which brought out *What Do People Do All Day* in 1968 and *Richard Scarry's Great Big Schoolhouse* in 1969.

But no matter for whom he writes, he is faithful to the novel and encyclopedic approach which he first used in *The Best Word Book Ever.* "When Scarry depicts houses, foods, trucks, boats, etc., he provides so many specific varieties within the general category that he usually manages to hit the very truck, house or boat that speaks volumes to any given small viewer," says Selma G. Lanes. "This probably explains why so many young children will pore over his busy, narrative illustrations, by themselves, for unnaturally long periods of time."

Another reason for their popularity is that the Scarry books have something of the runaway appeal of the comics. "In most of my books, you can follow the pictures one after the other, basically the same as you would a comic strip," Scarry says. Children like action and the comics give them plenty. And so does Richard Scarry.

The author-illustrator's personal life is as active and cheerful as his books. Up to 1967, he worked in the third-floor studio of his home in Westport, a little Connecticut town favored by writers and artists. His son, Richard, attended local schools, and Scarry and his wife were active in community affairs. Occasionally there were forays to New York City to consult publishers or visit theaters.

As one of Scarry's hobbies is skiing, he and his son spent the Christmas vacation of 1967 in Switzerland. "It was the usual 21-day excursion," he told Arthur Bell, who interviewed him for *Publishers Weekly*. "But coming home we had to pass through Lausanne to catch our plane from Geneva. From the train window I caught a glimpse of a child throwing a snowball—just that, nothing more—and I thought, 'Now is the time to move to Switzerland.' "

Subleasing their Westport home, the Scarrys moved to Lausanne, a town built entirely in steps, with a cathedral on its summit. Here, in their large, sunny apartment, they are close to Lake Geneva, and not far from Vevey, Montreux, and Morges, where celebrities from many fields make their homes; among them are Charlie Chaplin, James Mason, and Peter Ustinov.

Scarry himself is a local celebrity, with his books on display in the local stores. When Arthur Bell visited him, they dropped in at the neighborhood bookshop and were amused to see a solemn little girl, engrossed in a French edition of a Scarry book.

Writing conditions are as favorable for the author-illustrator as they were in Westport—and more picturesque. He has a pleasant studio (really the first apartment the family occupied) in the old quarter of Lausanne, where all the houses are decorated with murals, inside and out. "Not three hundred yards away from my studio is a meadow with sheep grazing in it," Scarry wrote to his publisher. "Just five minutes by car and I'm in cow country!"

Five minutes away are all the resources of a well-stocked bookstore, the Librairie Payot, which sells books in French, German, and English. Alongside the wall, in a basement annex, are stools for children, who are encouraged to come in and browse among the books on the shelves.

Because he is an enthusiastic traveler, his present location delights Richard Scarry. There is easy access to a number of countries. He can go to Milan to deliver his artwork to photo-offset plants, have lunch in Italy, and be home in Lausanne for dinner. A plane takes him to London or Paris in a couple of hours.

Although he hankers to do more traveling, his work is too demanding to permit more than weekends in the Swiss Alps or a skiing trip to Zermatt. Besides writing and illustrating his own books, he also illustrates for other writers. Altogether he has illustrated about eighty books since 1947.

His own books have a phenomenal sales record; over 25 million have been sold in the United States alone. "As aficionados of Mr. Scarry's work know," writes Janet Malcolm in *Something About the Author,* "his large, thick, colorful volumes, crammed with pictures and text, are loved by young children as no other modern picture books are loved."

JOAN WALSH ANGLUND

$\mathcal{T}$ODAY'S JUVENILE books come in many sizes and shapes. The more distinguished are conservative in format. The less distinguished sometimes try so hard for novelty that they become "gimmicky," even using shapes like bunnies, boats, or telephones.

Actually, small readers do not worry much about size or shape. They enjoy books which are so large that they are best read sprawled on the floor. But they also like tiny books; there is something cozy about a book which can be carried around easily or slipped under a pillow for bedtime reading.

Joan Walsh Anglund, whose books fall into two distinct types, uses sizes which are precisely suited to her subject matter. For adventure tales like *The Brave Cowboy* she chooses a size which shows off the large illustrations. But for such gentle statements as *A Friend Is Someone Who Likes You,* she turns to the diminutive format which Beatrix Potter made popular with her *Peter Rabbit* tales.

For the fullest enjoyment, these tiny books are perhaps best when read aloud by a grown-up who can explain and enlarge upon the text. Some adults, including some reviewers, have objected that these treasurable little books are not really suitable for children. And there is some truth in the criticism. While adults find the text warm and perceptive, small readers may find it difficult to understand what the author is telling them in such passages as:

> For the heart
> is its own world
> and in that world
> you are important!

But whether they fully understand them or not, young readers love the books of Joan Walsh Anglund, reveling in the miniature world which the author-illustrator presents with such quaintness and charm.

Joan Walsh Anglund was born in 1926, in Hinsdale, Illinois, and grew up in Hinsdale and Evanston. The latter, a beautiful city on Lake Michigan, is graciously planned with tree-lined streets, open spaces, and colleges set in ample grounds. Later in life, Joan was often homesick for the greenness and openness of Evanston; she found its people and environment far more sympathetic than those of the other urban communities in which she was temporarily obliged to live.

Joan grew up in a family to whom art was important. Her mother was a gifted amateur artist. Although she gave up painting when her children were small, her flower pictures and landscapes hung on the walls of the Walsh home, a source of inspiration to her children. Joan's father, a commercial artist, was always ready to encourage her early efforts. "I remember a day when he was hurrying off to Chicago," she says. "He already had his coat on—but he stopped when I asked him how to draw a bow. I wanted to draw a doll with a very special dress, trimmed with a ribbon bow. He showed me how to give it dimension and how to 'shade' the sides to make it look round and full."

Like her mother's, her father's art work was in evidence all around the house, so that Joan grew up believing that drawing was the natural way to express oneself. "I remember being surprised when I went to friends' houses and discovered that not *all* parents drew or painted," she says.

The sudden death of her much loved father when she was ten, and the earlier death of her baby sister, Barbara Joy, led Joan to ponder the meaning of life and its mystery earlier than most children do. Her pondering eventually led to tranquil daydreaming and to stretches of happy solitude when she often wanted nothing more than to watch the drifting clouds or the play of light on trees and flowers. Today, as mother and grandmother, she feels sorry for modern children, rushed as they often are into too many planned activities. She believes that all youngsters, especially those who are creative, should be allowed plenty of time for their own pursuits, for imagining, for dreaming, and for getting to know and understand themselves.

Though she enjoyed spells of solitude, Joan was a friendly child, ready to share her interests with her friends. (When she learned to make that bow, she drew endless bows for her admiring classmates.) A gentle, rather shy child, she was a follower rather than a leader. In particular, she loved to follow where her sister Patsy led. "My sister was my first and best friend," she says. "I depended on her for almost everything. One day, when we were buying ice cream, I said, 'What kind of ice cream do I want today, Patsy?' Needless to say, the episode became a family joke—my children still tease me about it."

It was Patsy who taught Joan to love ballet and art and poetry, and who, when they were older, discussed with her such debatable subjects as evolution and extra sensory perception. "Patsy has a probing mind. She's very direct, whereas I'm apt to be a bit dreamy," Joan says.

Different in character and temperament, the sisters complemented each other to perfection. They remain close; today, proud of Joan's success, Patsy helps her with the paper work and correspondence which her career involves, and sometimes discusses story ideas with her.

Although she early showed a talent for drawing, there seemed little prospect that Joan could attend art school. What little money the family possessed had to be stretched to cover the education of both girls. But Joan was fortunate. Mary McMullen, her high-school art teacher, announced one day that she had secured a scholarship for her talented pupil; actually, she was using her savings to help Joan.

After studying at the School of the Chicago Art Institute and the American Academy of Art, Joan became an apprentice in the studio of Adele Roth, a well-known commercial artist. She planned to go into fashion design, but Adele steered her away from it. Recognizing Joan's special gifts, she suggested that book illustrating would be a better field for her.

Retiring by nature, Joan was not career-minded. When, in 1947, she married Bob Anglund, she was quite content to move to Pasadena and settle down as a housewife. Her drawing, she thought, would be a pleasant avocation.

While her husband worked in radio and the theater, she buried herself in happy domesticity. She might have stopped at being a housewife had she not received a nudge in the right direction. When they moved back to Evanston her daughter, Joy, was born, and Joan realized that extra money would not come amiss. So she began to do some free-lance illustrating, although with no feeling of pressure.

When the little family, which by now included a son, Todd, moved to Forest Hills, New York, Joan was unhappy. She found it difficult to turn an apartment into the kind of home she wanted to give her family, a home with beauty and individuality. And her children, instead of being able to romp in a park, now had nothing but a concrete playground. Joan herself missed her friends in Evanston, which she still considered home. Joy, too, longed for the playmates she had left behind.

One day, as she watched her children playing, Joan was reflecting on her loneliness. Suddenly a definition of friendship flashed into her mind. "A friend is someone who loves you," she thought. She scribbled the sentence down forthwith and expanded the idea, thoughts and words coming almost effortlessly. When she returned to the apartment she put the little composition away, never dreaming that it was to become the text of her first book.

Although she did some book illustrating at this time, she made little attempt to "push" her work, much less think of becoming an author-illustrator. It was her husband who took steps to start her toward a career. He encouraged her to make a dummy of the kind of book she thought she would like to write. Joan remembered the text about friendship that she had tucked away; now she took it out, illustrated it, and made a dummy book.

When Bob Anglund showed it to Margaret McElderry,

then juvenile editor at Harcourt, Brace and World, that perceptive editor recognized that the little book was perfect as it stood. It was published in 1958.

To the surprise of its modest author-illustrator, *A Friend Is Someone Who Likes You* was a runaway success. Recommended by word of mouth, it quickly became a best seller and people of all ages rushed to buy it—for themselves, for friends, for gift-giving. They delighted in its diminutive format, its delicate, pastel-colored pictures, and its Edwardian charm. But most of all they liked it because it echoed their own sentiments—and echoed them with appealing warmth and simplicity.

During the next few years, Joan Walsh Anglund wrote three more books of the same kind; *Love Is a Special Way of Feeling, Christmas Is a Time of Giving,* and *Spring Is a New Beginning.* Like her first book, they enchanted a great variety of readers and became best sellers.

Joan did not, however, confine her work to books of this very special kind. She also wrote books which were specifically designed for children. *Cowboy and His Friend, Cowboy's Secret,* and others, were straightforward adventure tales, filled with action and imagination. She also illustrated her own version of the Hansel and Gretel story, *Nibble Nibble Mousekin,* and brought out a collection of her gay and amusing poems for children, *Morning Is a Little Child.*

The artwork in her two types of book differs as widely as the subject matter. In her tiny books the pictures are delicate, soft-hued, with amusing original touches. (The little characters, for instance, have dots for eyes and undefined features, yet their faces are surprisingly expressive—wistful, curious, dreamy, amused.) In the *Cowboy* books, the illustra-

135

tions are sharp and vigorous, with vivid colors and plenty of lively humor.

Today, and for some time past, Joan Walsh Anglund has enjoyed an ideal environment in which to work and live. She has the kind of home she always envisioned—a lovely old house with a garden, trees, and birds. Located in Westport, Connecticut, it satisfies her love of the unusual; the house was once an inn and the kitchen is converted from a blacksmith's forge.

She and her husband, always her most helpful and understanding critic, share many interests besides her work. They enjoy the theater in all its forms, ballet, and travel. Among other countries, they have visited Russia, Japan, Sweden, France, and their favorite, England.

Three of the Anglunds are collectors. Joan and Joy collect dolls, dollhouses, and nostalgic accessories. Bob prefers antique circus wagons, clown figures, and kindred items. Todd is not a collector; he is a very promising young artist—"his huge canvases are slowly filling up the house!" Joan says.

But Joan's major interest is still the writing and illustrating of books. A minor interest is the novelties which her books inspire—dolls, date pads illustrated with gay Anglund figures, picture samplers, etc.

To her joy, for she is deeply interested in people of all kinds, her books continue to attract thousands of readers of all types and ages. Some of her work has traveled far afield. *A Friend Is Someone Who Likes You* has been published in Norway, Denmark, England, Sweden and Germany, and has appeared in French as *Un Ami C'est Quelqu'un Qui T'aime*. *Love Is a Special Way of Feeling* has even been translated into Latin (*Amor Est Sensus Quidam Peculiaris*).

Perhaps the universal appeal of these books lies in the fact that they are pertinent to our times. Today we are being called upon to make special efforts in the cause of brotherhood; we are urged to be tolerant, to care about our neighbor, to love, to share. And the Anglund books, with their emphasis on kindness, understanding, and the gentler virtues, are telling reminders of what we need to do.

MAURICE SENDAK

$\mathcal{M}$AURICE SENDAK is surely the only author-illustrator who insists that his art springs from toys, comic books—and Mickey Mouse. "This is the art I grew up with," he told writer Saul Braun. "It is what made me. The comics and Mickey Mouse."

Recently he proved this to his satisfaction. He was showing *Where the Wild Things Are* to a friend, a film collector. Amused, she brought out a still from an early horror movie, *King Kong,* and held it beside one of the illustrations, a monster emerging from a cave. The illustration, Maurice says, was "literally, a copy. But I had not seen the still, of course. . . . Obviously it (the film) had impressed itself on my mind, and there it was."

Perhaps Maurice Sendak's work is so gratifying to children just because of its debt to the comics, the movies, and the preposterous little animals they love. Adults find a nightmarish quality in some of Sendak's books, but children are in their element.

Maurice Sendak was born on June 10, 1928, in Brooklyn, New York. His parents immigrated from Poland before World War One. Philip Sendak, father of Natalie, Jack, and Maurice, was a dressmaker who prospered in his new country, sharing a shop with his partners on New York City's bustling 34th Street. Although he had a financial setback at the time of Maurice's birth, he was able to provide a comfortable home for his children and—more important—give them a good share of his time and attention.

Maurice, the youngest, was delicate, imaginative, and impressionable, reacting strongly to people and places. He found some of the family visitors "extremely ugly," and the memory may have been reflected in his drawings of pugnacious youngsters and oddly shaped grown-ups. He "feels" rather than remembers his childhood and is more interested in conveying this feeling than in anatomical accuracy.

He did not shrink from ugliness or abnormality; it may even have attracted him. "My best friend was the girl next door. She was somewhat retarded," he told Saul Braun. "Her sister was retarded, too, and had polio. I wrote a long, unpublished book about that child. She is a rat in it."

As a small boy, perhaps because of his parents' concern over his frequent illnesses, Maurice was often preoccupied with the thought of death. Later, in *Pierre,* he tells of a little boy who defies death. "I don't care," he says. Even after he is gobbled up by a lion, Pierre still doesn't care.

Maurice's childhood, however, was not all fears and gloom. There were his sister and brother to tag after. There were things to see, and he early showed pleasure in the pictorial. Once, when he was convalescing, his grandmother sat him on her knee by the window. To amuse him, she pulled the shade up and down. Maurice was enthralled. "I was thrilled by the sudden reappearance of the backyard every time the shade went up, the falling snow, and my brother and sister busy constructing a sooty snowman."

He was fortunate in his parents. Sarah, his mother, was a

woman of warmth and vitality, devoted to her little son, although she did not always understand him. She provided him with a variety of backgrounds. In those days, apartment-dwellers easily found a new place to live. Sarah Sendak moved her family often, snatching Maurice from schools and friends so that there was always something different to see, something new to adapt to.

Maurice's fervid imagination was inherited from his father. Philip Sendak was a splendid storyteller, although his tales were sometimes scary. Instead of a nightly pillow fight, he told his children "continued stories," improvising as he went along.

One of these Maurice characteristically hankers to retell. It was about a little boy who wandered away from his parents. As the snow fell, he huddled under a tree, weeping with cold and misery. Suddenly a monstrous figure loomed over him. A voice said, "I am Abraham, your father." Sarah, too, appeared and the small boy was comforted. But when his parents found him, he was dead.

The first books Maurice owned, mostly comics, were printed on cheap paper and had slapdash illustrations in gaudy colors. But although he learned to pretend to despise them, he could not forget them. "They weren't fancy, they were good," he told Virginia Haviland, a librarian. His *In the Night Kitchen* was an attempt to make a beautiful book which still suggested the inexpensive, exciting books of his childhood.

He wanted to be an illustrator very early in life. At first he simply copied his brother Jack, who was always writing and illustrating stories (and who later became the author of *Circus Girl* and *The Happy Rain,* which Maurice illustrated).

But at nine he began to make up his own stories, hand-lettering them, illustrating them, and binding them into little books with decorative covers. He found, too, that he had his father's gift for story-telling and could count on a fascinated audience of neighborhood boys and girls when he told stories from the films of Walt Disney.

Maurice went to high school during World War Two, and he hated it. Drawing was the only subject that attracted him, but there was no real instruction so he went his own way. "I practically drew my way through school," he says. After school, and on weekends, he worked for All American Comics, a comic book syndicate, where he relished his job of adapting Mutt and Jeff strips, laying out the pages, filling in backgrounds, and extending the story line when necessary.

After graduation, he was employed by Timely Service, a window-display firm. Here again, the world of fantasy absorbed him. He helped to construct such figures as Snow White and the Seven Dwarfs out of chicken wire, papier maché, spun glass, paper, and paint.

During the summer of 1948, he and Jack built six animated wooden toys which they took to F.A.O. Schwartz, the famous Fifth Avenue toystore. "The pieces, five of which Sendak now has in his studio, are in the tradition of the 18th century German lever-operated toys," Nat Hentoff wrote in a profile of Maurice Sendak in *The New Yorker*. "When a lever is pulled, for instance, a ferocious wolf leaps out of bed and Little Red Riding Hood collapses."

The display director at Schwartz's was impressed, although he explained that the figures would be too expensive to mass-produce. He hired Maurice, who stayed with the store for three years, attending the Art Students League in the evenings.

Ursula Nordstrom, far-seeing editor of Harper Junior Books, gave Maurice his first opportunity in professional illustrating. She invited him to do the pictures for Marcel Aymé's *The Wonderful Farm*. But his highly individual style came into its own when he illustrated Ruth Krauss' *A Hole Is to Dig*, which appeared in 1952. A book of definitions, it gets down to basics in the most diverting way. "Buttons are to keep people warm." "A cat is so you can have kittens." "A dream is to look at the night and see things." In the illustrations, Maurice Sendak's tubby little people are exactly right, and wonderfully self-important.

With *Kenny's Window*, 1946, Maurice began to write and illustrate his own books. Kenny, wistful and timorous, sets out to find the answers to seven questions, put to him by a rooster in a dream. "What is an only goat?" "What is a Very Narrow Escape?" "Do you always want what you think you want?" After a jaunt to Switzerland and other dream escapades, Kenny is able to answer the questions with insouciance. *Kenny's Window* was an Honor Book in the *New York Herald Tribune*'s 1956 Children's Spring Book Festival.

Further honors, and an outburst of controversy, greeted *Where the Wild Things Are,* which won the Caldecott Medal in 1964. In this picture book, small Max is sent to bed for misbehavior. He runs away to his private world of horned and scaly monsters, whom he dominates by looking them unblinkingly in the eye. A "wild rumpus" has Max and the monsters hanging from trees, baying at the moon, capering, and cavorting. But monsters, although satisfying to certain moods, do not have the warm reality of human beings. So Max eventually returns home, to find supper waiting for him on the table.

Librarians, while admitting the startling originality of the monster-characters, had reservations about *Where the Wild Things Are*. Maurice, however, was unworried. With the Caldecott Medal as his justification, he determined to write other books in the same vein, books that would show his "involvement with the inescapable fact of childhood—the awful vulnerability of children and their struggle to make themselves king of all wild things."

In his next book, however, the illustrations of animals have a tender and touching quality, and Jennie, the dog, is completely lovable. His pet Sealyham, she had often appeared in his work, but *Higglety Pigglety Pop!* is Jenny's own book, dedicated to her. Based on a Mother Goose rhyme, it is an elaborate modern fairy tale. Deciding that "there must be more to life," Jennie packs her gold-buckled black leather bag and goes off to find something she does not already have.

She has adventures, sometimes hair-raising to the reader, which she takes imperturbably. To save the baby whom she is nursemaiding, she even sticks her head into a lion's mouth. "Please eat me," she says, "I need the experience anyway." Perhaps Jennie doesn't quite mean this, because she saves herself in time and the book ends with her debut as leading lady of The World Mother Goose Theatre in "Higglety Pigglety Pop!"

With *In the Night Kitchen,* 1970, Maurice Sendak carried out his intention of making a good book which would nonetheless suggest the popular art of his childhood. Children reveled in it, but among adults the book created something of a furor. They objected to the totally naked, pink small boy who, by the light of the moon, falls into the bakers' dough pan. Temporarily dressed in dough, Mickey rollicks over the Milky Way in the night kitchen, falls into a bottle of milk, and emerges, pink and naked again, to help with the batter. Mickey is wholly ingratiating. "If he could corrupt the morals of anyone, child or adult," says Arto De-Mirjian, Jr., in an article in *Publishers Weekly,* "he or she would have to come from another planet."

A bachelor, Mr. Sendak lived for some years in a Manhattan duplex, filled with recordings, first editions, paintings, and the toys and gadgets which he uses as props for his illustrations.

Recently, he moved to Connecticut, where he works and gardens and is "even more happily isolated." For company he has two dogs, a Golden Retriever and a German Shepherd. Having renounced the duplex, he keeps a small cooperative apartment in Greenwich Village for when he needs to stay in the city. Dedicated to his work, he seldom interrupts it, except to consult with his editor, work out in a gym, or fly to Europe to accept an award.

Besides the Caldecott Medal, Maurice Sendak has won many other honors, including the International Hans Christian Andersen Awards Illustrator's Medal, presented every two years to an illustrator whose works have made an outstanding contribution to children's literature. The first American to win this award, he has illustrated over sixty books, more than thirty of which have been published abroad.

His work has been compared with that of Edward Lear, and of Sir John Tenniel, the illustrator of *Alice in Wonderland.* Maurice has something of the grotesque and wayward

humor of Lear; something of the crisp, cool fantasy of Tenniel. *Time* magazine has called him "the Picasso of children's books," a title open to question. It is doubtful
whether many children like or appreciate Picasso. But there
is no doubt whatever that children everywhere both relish
and understand the works of Maurice Sendak.

TOMI UNGERER

ALTHOUGH HE HAS adopted America as his country, author-illustrator Tomi Ungerer looks back with pride upon a native land of unusual beauty, rich in tradition. Alsace-Lorraine is a charming and colorful French province, with pink houses and storks resting on the roofs. But its people have seldom been left in peace. Time and time again they have had to abandon their fields and vineyards for the sterile and destructive ways of war. This has produced a character which often seems contradictory and unpredictable.

A true Alsatian, Tomi Ungerer was born on October 28, 1931, in Strasbourg, the capital of the province. A medieval fortress city, it is rich in history. In the Middle Ages, it was part of the Holy Roman Empire, but since then it has often changed hands. In 1870, Strasbourg surrendered to the Germans, but after World War One it passed again to France. During World War Two, with the collapse of the French in 1940, the city was once more lost to Germany.

The young Tomi grew up in a Nazi-occupied city, reacting strongly, if unconsciously, to an alien presence. To this fact, biographer John Gruen attributes the adult Tomi's "black humor." "As a child in his native Strasbourg, he (Tomi) was brainwashed by Nazi schoolteachers, in one of whose classes the first assignment was to draw a caricature of a Jew. It struck Ungerer as a somewhat peculiar assignment, and it led to certain germinal insights—one of the most important being that to expose something to satire is, in effect, to kill it. And so Ungerer the child began to expose—in his fashion." Tomi himself tells how he began to draw "the most outrageous things. Terrible, bloody, fearful things."

As a result, the art of Tomi Ungerer today has two sides, strikingly opposed. In his adult work—posters, paintings, cartoons, advertising—he is bitingly satiric, revealing his contempt for the greed, cruelty, and corruption too often hidden under a facade of "niceness." The purpose of his satire is to produce a better world. His books for children are wholly different; the tales and drawings are captivating in their sheer fun, their spirit of innocence and wonder. There is tenderness, too, and compassion. In *I Am Papa Snap and These Are My Favorite None Such Tales,* he shows Mr. Limpid pushing his wife in her wheelchair.

> Mr. Limpid is blind.
> Mrs. Limpid is lame.
> They are old.
> They are happy.
> They love each other.

Juxtaposed is a quietly ludicrous picture of Mrs. Morsel, driving a steamroller through her living room.

> Mr. Maroon Morsel gave his wife Retina a steamroller
> for their twentieth anniversary.
> She uses it to iron out her laundry
> and flatten pizza dough.
> They drive it on weekends to visit Mr. Morsel's
> bedridden mother who lives in the mountains.

In a city famous for its metal and machinery manufactures, the Ungerers were watchmakers. Tomi did not follow the family occupation, although he probably inherited the meticulous care with which he works. In "A Visit to Tomi Ungerer," Joan Hess Michell describes his studio at the time. "The large windows which open to the terrace are decorated with line drawings of female figures. In the corner near the desk stands Tomi's drawing board. Brushes, pens and ink, crayons, paints, pencils—all are neatly arranged. His working area is very businesslike; no nonsense here."

During his late teens, Tomi was impressed by the cartoons and illustrations in *The New Yorker,* copies of which came his way during the American occupation of Alsace-Lorraine. He hoped some day to draw in that style. His formal art training was brief; he studied for a year at Strasbourg's *Art Decoratif* and spent some time in Paris. But he felt that he would gain more experience on his own, and set out to walk and hitchhike through Europe, "the best way to travel, meet people, and have adventures." He did his military service in an unusual branch of the French Mounted Police, a camel caravan in the Algerian Sahara.

In 1956, he came to New York City, prepared to make his home in America. Taking samples of his work, he called on publishers, eventually getting a hearing at Harper and Row. With her usual percipience, editor Ursula Nordstrom recognized an out-of-the-way talent and started him on his first children's book, *The Mellops Go Flying.* The tale of a remarkable family of French pigs, who do everything with finesse, it was an Honor Book in the 1957 *New York Herald Tribune*'s Children's Spring Book Festival.

Though busy as well with various forms of adult art,

Tomi found time for a variety of pursuits, among them archeology, mineralogy, geology, even spelunking. The excellent reception given to his first book led inevitably to more Mellop books, in which the bland little pigs reflected Tomi's activities. *The Mellops Go Diving for Treasure* appeared in 1957; *The Mellops Strike Oil,* in 1958; *Christmas Eve with the Mellops,* in 1960. *The Mellops Go Spelunking,* 1963, shows the family following an underground river, marveling at stalactites and stalagmites.

> "Look! Icicles, but of stone," called Ferdinand.
> "Mother's cream pie," said Casimir.
> "Pillars as in a cathedral," exclaimed Felix.
> "And pipe organs," called Isidor.

They trace cave paintings, dig up artifacts, and have a satisfying adventure with smugglers. All is brilliantly pictured in black, blue, and pink.

Tomi's small daughter Phoebe, in whom he delights, has sparked many of his ideas. With her as inspiration, he designed and developed a group of playground toys, similar to those in Sweden's famous "adventure playgrounds." On these the children can climb, balance, play follow-my-leader, or imagine themselves anything they wish.

Like Maurice Sendak, Tomi enjoys creating strange figures. In his studio, says Joan Hess Michell in *The American Artist,* "low shelves house what Tomi describes as his inventions: humorous figures of animals, cleverly made from unlikely odds and ends of common household objects. Two rusted tin cans are transformed into a comical hippopotamus; a few sticks and chips of wood become a long-legged bird; a discarded beer can forms the body of a mouse; a light bulb becomes his head."

During a summer on Long Island, Tomi became fascinated with kites. Remembering the thrill of a childhood pastime in Strasbourg, he bought a small kite, flew it, and succumbed to the magic of kites and kiteflying. Before the summer was over, he had designed and made more than a hundred kites of all sizes and shapes, with acrylic-painted designs.

The windswept beaches of East Hampton proved irresistible. Tomi could not get enough of his new hobby. For three winters, working with professional skill, he experimented with kites. James W. Wagenvoord, in *Flying Kites*, tells how "Tomi Ungerer's kites have often confused bathers on the long, rolling stretches of sand. With wet algae hanging from the string, the kite slips down over a dozing sunbather until the algae sweeps across the bather's back. Then, with a pull of the string, the kite is sent shooting up into the air, leaving a bewildered vacationer trying to figure out what has happened."

As energetic and versatile in his work as in his hobbies, Tomi is against specializing. "There is no communication of artists today," he told Joan Hess Michell, "as there was in the Renaissance. Then artists tried all phases of work. I don't want to be called just an illustrator or an author. I am striving ideally (and perhaps it is unobtainable) to be a Renaissance man. I do anything I am interested in; I do what I want to do artistically."

So he illustrates for such leading publications as *McCalls*, *Esquire*, and *Holiday*. He designs eye-catching posters with brief, compelling text for *The New York Times*, the *Village*

Voice, and the New York lottery. He undertakes special projects that pique his interest. For Expo '67 he designed a section of the United States and Canadian pavilions, and did posters and promotion. His movie company, Wild Oats, produced a weekly TV program for the Canadian Broadcasting Company.

But, as he himself realizes, work of this kind is ephemeral. His fame is likely to rest on his children's books, which continue to surprise and delight. Tireless in invention, he has something of Maurice Sendak's love for improbable creatures: in his books, of the same name, *Crictor* is a boa constrictor; *Emile* is an octopus; *Orlando,* a vulture—but a brave one; *Rufus* is a bat who wants to be a beautifully colored moth; *Adelaide* is a kangaroo—with wings.

Leaving the world of zany animals, Tomi turned, in 1967, to conceive Moon Man, an up-to-the-minute, gently satiric fable for children. Moon Man, round, soft looking, and pertinently green (for is not the moon made of green cheese?) was bored in the sky. He caught the tip of a comet's tail, flew to earth, and was captured and thrown into jail. But "every night as the moon grew thinner and thinner so did the Moon Man until at last he was able to squeeze through the bars of his window." After many adventures, he meets Doctor Bunsen van der Dunkel, a 300-year-old scientist who has just perfected a spacecraft. The Doctor asks Moon Man to be his first passenger and "the Moon Man, who had realized he could never live peacefully on this planet, agreed to go." He waits until he enters his third quarter and is small enough to fit into the capsule. Then he blasts off "with a roar of rockets," never to return.

Tomi works in a variety of media, and his style in everything he produces is continually changing. He uses pen and ink, oil and water colors, chalk, crayon, charcoal, tempera. "I enjoy trying different ways of expression to break the monotony," he says. He often designs as well as illustrates his books, and sometimes experiments with special type or calligraphy.

Tomi Ungerer has received awards in all branches of his work (and even his hobbies have won recognition, several of his original kites being on display at the Hallmark Gallery in New York City). The Society of Illustrators awarded him a gold medal in 1960. *Crictor, Emile,* and *Snail, Where Are You?* have all been Honor books in the *New York Herald Tribune*'s Children's Spring Book Festival. *Zerelda's Ogre* and *The Moon Man* both appeared on *Time* magazine's list of Best Reading for children of three to six. Ungerer's complete works have been exhibited at the American Institute of Graphic Arts where they excited considerable interest and admiration.

INDEX